BOURBON
AT ITS BEST

*The Lore & Allure
of America's Finest Spirits*

BOURBON
AT ITS BEST

The Lore & Allure
of America's Finest Spirits

R O N   G I V E N S

For further information, please contact the publisher at:

 Clerisy Press
1700 Madison Road
Cincinnati, OH 45206
www.clerisypress.com

Library of Congress Cataloging-in-Publication Data

Givens, Ron, 1950–
    Bourbon at its best: the lore & allure of America's finest spirits/
        by Ron Givens.
    p. cm.
    Includes index.
    ISBN-13: 978-1578-60304-6
    ISBN-10: 1-57860-304-8
    1. Whiskey. I. Title.
    TP605.G58 2005
    641.2'52—dc22

                        2005016265

Produced by Menasha Ridge Press
Distributed by Publishers Group West
Cover and interior designed by Alian Design
Cover photo by Chris Bryant
Printed in Canada
First edition, first printing

ABOUT THE AUTHOR

Ron Givens has written extensively about spirits and beer for such publications as the *New York Daily News*, *Newsweek*, *Time Out New York*, and *Drinks* magazine. His work has also appeared in *People*, *Entertainment Weekly*, *Rolling Stone*, and *Ladies' Home Journal*.

ABOUT THE AUTHOR

Ron Givens has written extensively about spirits and beer for such publications as the *New York Daily News*, *Newsweek*, *Time Out New York*, and *Drinks* magazine. His work has also appeared in *People*, *Entertainment Weekly*, *Rolling Stone*, and *Ladies' Home Journal*.

THE SMOOTH CROON OF BOURBON
A Polite Introduction

Booker Noe was a big man in bourbon, and not just because he stood six feet four. No, Noe gained his stature in the distilling business through a combination of birthright and hard work. He was the grandson of a whiskey-making legend, Jim Beam, who was himself the grandson of a whiskey-making legend, Jacob Beam, who was the man who got the family into distilling in the first place. Noe expanded upon this genetic advantage while running the Beam operation from 1965 till 1992, making it the leading producer of bourbon in the world, and then while promoting it by acting as a brand ambassador up until his death in 2004, at the age of 74.

When I met him, underneath a tent set up about a half mile from the tall distill-

ing house that anchors the world of Beam, Noe had been slowed physically, but his personality still had the strength and tang of the spirit he loved so greatly. We were part of a group eating heartily from a large buffet and washing it all down with a selection of Jim Beam whiskeys. (Well, maybe a few people were sipping lemonade.) Noe sat to my right, and his wife, Annis, sat to his right. There were others at the table, but they were, like I was, spectators at a lively, unforced performance. Booker Noe was a country ham, and the fact that he very well knew it did not diminish the pleasure of his company. My favorite moment in the conversation came when Noe remembered the very first time he tasted bourbon, as a young

The recent boom in finer bourbon has placed greater emphasis on aging in oak barrels for longer periods of time, and that gives the finished whiskeys a wider and deeper range of flavors.

boy. "I went around and collected the tears from bottles," he said, referring to the small drips from what were, essentially, empties. "And then I took it out to the privy, and then I swallowed it." Noe paused, his eyes widening: "It *boie-ee-ee-en-nn-nd!*"

Thankfully, for all who enjoy fine bourbon, Noe was not discouraged. In 1988, about 50 years after this primal experience, he created a namesake bourbon—Booker's—which became part of a new product line from Jim Beam four years later. The Small Batch Bourbon Collection—which also included Knob Creek, Basil Hayden's, and Baker's—kick-started the market for better bourbon. Beam may not have begun this trend—in 1984 Elmer T. Lee, master distiller of what was then the Ancient Age Distillery, brought out a single-barrel product called Blanton's—but the marketing clout of Beam, then and now the top-selling bourbon in the world, provided a great boost. Since the late 1980s, more than 50 high-end whiskeys have been introduced. Some of them, like the Beam products, are blends of finer whiskeys in batches that are smaller than the ones used for more affordable spirits. Other high-end bourbons are unblended bottlings from single barrels that have been identified as quite special.

Over the course of the 1990s, the response to these exceptional bourbons has been strong and steady, outstripping demand for standard bottlings. While sales of basic bourbons were relatively flat at the turn of the 21st century, sales of small-batch and single-barrel bourbons doubled over one five-year stretch. That fits into a broader trend of budding connoisseurship. Americans have developed a taste for pricier spirits in general, whether they are single-malt whiskies from Scotland, deluxe vodkas from Poland, or those rich elixirs from the northwestern corner of Kentucky that take their name from a county where they are not, in fact, legally made at all: bourbon.

Nowadays, bourbon lovers are in hog heaven. They can go into a store and savor a wide range of choices. But which choice to make? What is the difference, for example, between the Evan Williams Single Barrel Vintage 1994 and the Evan Williams Single Barrel Vintage 1995? Or among Old Bardstown, Old Forester, Old Charter, Old Ezra, Old Rip Van Winkle, Old Weller, Very Old Barton, and Very Special Old Fitzgerald? Considering the prices for these bourbons— quite reasonable compared with other premium spirits, but not cheap— people don't want to plunk their money down on a whim. And believe me, there are considerable, and very enjoyable, differences from one bourbon to the next. One man's (or woman's) Wild Turkey Russell's Reserve is not another woman's (or man's) Maker's Mark.

That's why this book exists: to help you sort through a world of difficult, wonderful decisions. You'll come to appreciate the distinctive qualities of every small-batch and single-barrel bourbon on the market in the most comprehensive survey of bourbon in years. You'll understand the different ways that bourbon is made and how each step in the process—and each ingredient—contributes to flavor and smoothness. You'll find out how bourbon has changed over time, from its roots in the soil of American farms to its down-home image as good old "likker" to its rather exalted present status as one of the world's finer libations. You'll learn the different ways to enjoy this spirit in cocktails, from the "old-fashioned" to the newfangled. And you'll see how you can visit the colorful and down-to-earth distilleries that give us such drinking pleasure. Whether you are a newcomer or whether you're steeped in branch water, this book will increase your enjoyment of America's favorite whiskey.

My own understanding of bourbon came of age with the introduction of these boutique brands. My mother's father may have had a preference for Four Roses bourbon, but I never saw him take a sip—my mother's mother did not approve, so there were no tears for me. My mother managed a liquor shop in an Omaha, Nebraska, department store, but she barely touched any of her wares, so my appreciation of the fancy bottles and decanters that contained bourbon never extended to the actual contents inside them. As

By law, barrels can be used only once to age bourbon, but they still have a lot to offer, so they're used to age everything from single malts in Scotland to rum in Jamaica to tequila in Mexico.

a student at Iowa State University, sitting in its football stadium, I drank a little (maybe sometimes a lot of) Jim Beam and Coca-Cola to numb the pain caused by the cold and the woeful athleticism on the field. My informed sense of bourbon has developed over the past ten years, as I have sampled the exquisite spirits that have entered the marketplace in increasing numbers. I have been surprised, intrigued, enraptured, dazzled, tantalized, thrilled, awestruck, sated, content. But I can honestly say I have never been boie-ee-ee-en-nn-nd.

So, grab your glass and come along. We're about to have some *fun*.

Cheers,

Charcoal mellowing distinguishes Tennessee whiskeys from Kentucky bourbons.

HOW BOURBON IS MADE
A Spirit Born in Dust

Grain, water, yeast, and wood—these are the four elements
that come together in the production of bourbon whiskey.
The first three do their job in the span of a week or so,
but the fourth takes years to assert its influence.

Grain comes first. By law, the "mash-bill" (or combination of grains being used) for straight bourbon must contain at least 51 percent corn. The whiskey's basic sweetness, as well as some of its body, comes from the corn. The grain used is very similar to the stuff that gets turned into the cornmeal you buy in grocery stores. Most of this corn comes from Kentucky and surrounding states.

The second most prominent grain is either rye or wheat—what the industry calls small grains. By varying the amounts of the small grains, a distiller gets different flavors. Rye produces a whiskey that is spicier and fuller, while wheat makes it lighter and more mellow; the two are virtually never used together to make bourbon. The rye and wheat are generally grown in the upper Midwest or Canada.

Again, these grains resemble those used in common food products. For example, the soft winter wheat that goes into Maker's Mark—a whiskey known as a wheated bourbon—is the sort used for baking pastries, cakes, and cookies.

The third grain is barley in malted form, which provides enzymes that convert the starches in the other grains into sugars that can be fermented. The malting process begins with the soaking of barley grains to cause germination, which involves the sprouting of a tiny seedling. This converts starch in the barley to sugars that would otherwise feed the growth of a new plant.

But the people who produce malt—"maltsers," located primarily in the Midwest—arrest this development by drying out the grain with heat.

All of the grains are milled to a rather fine consistency; if you were to hold this grist in your hand, part of it would be like flour and part of it would be like cornmeal. The goal here is to make the grist easy to saturate with water so the fermentable sugars will be more readily absorbed into the water when cooked.

The second element, water, plays a more crucial role than you might think. Kentucky became the dominant place for bourbon in part because its water gets filtered naturally through limestone beneath the surface of the earth. After passing through the bedrock, this water is extremely low in iron and rich in two important

Limestone water brings out the best in malt and yeast.

minerals: calcium and magnesium. "A little bit of calcium and magnesium is very important to the yeast," says Jerry Dalton, master distiller for Jim Beam. "It makes the yeast get all healthy and robust and happy and want to do what little yeast cells do, which is to multiply."

There's another, quite dramatic effect if the water has not been stripped of iron. New spirit coming off the still is often diluted before going into barrels for aging, and if the water used has too much iron this element will react with chemicals in the wood, turning the whiskey anywhere from emerald green to coal black. Not willing to take chances, distilleries dilute their spirits only with water that has been demineralized.

MASHING

To make bourbon, first you make a thin porridge. It'll be a combination of corn and rye, or corn and wheat, and it's cooked with boiling water and steam under high pressure. The type of cooking vessel varies from distillery to distillery.

At the Buffalo Trace Distillery, corn and rye go together into huge, closed-off cylindrical vessels—essentially, industrial-strength pressure cookers. Steam brings the temperature to about 235 degrees, and the mash cooks for about 30 minutes. "This breaks the starch down into

All the grains used to make bourbon are cooked into a kind of porridge, which converts their sugars into liquid form, so yeast can feed upon them and create a beerlike form of alcohol.

soluble starch," says Elmer T. Lee, master distiller emeritus at Buffalo Trace. Then the mixture is cooled to about 150 degrees so that the malt can be added without damaging its enzymes. "This," Lee says, "converts the liquid starch into liquid sugar. Then you cool it down to 65 degrees and pump it into the fermenter."

At Woodford Reserve, which has open cookers, the process differs slightly. The corn is boiled at about 240 degrees; then the temperature is lowered to 180 degrees before the rye is added, and then the temperature is lowered to about 140 degrees before the malt goes in.

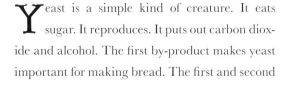 FERMENTATION

Yeast is a simple kind of creature. It eats sugar. It reproduces. It puts out carbon dioxide and alcohol. The first by-product makes yeast important for making bread. The first and second

make it important for making beer. But distillers want only the alcohol, and they work very hard to maintain the right strain of yeast for the flavors and aroma and body they seek.

These strains are very carefully nurtured and protected by distillers, who closely guard the "mother" yeast, even if that means keeping it refrigerated in an entirely different city. The Beam company, for example, works with the same strain of yeast that Jim Beam himself created when he reentered the distilling business after the end of Prohibition.

Chris Morris, master distiller at Brown-Forman, tells of a difficult time during Prohibition when the company was allowed to distill "medicinal" whiskey—actually, its Old Forester brand—on a limited basis but didn't have the yeast to do it. "We had to work hard to find a strain in 1929 to replicate Old Forester."

TENNESSEE
WHISKEY

Tennessee whiskey, like bourbon, is made from a combination of grains that includes more corn than anything else. The grains are milled, cooked, fermented, and distilled in ways that are very similar to those used to produce bourbon.

But once the whiskey in Tennessee comes out of the still, there is one crucial difference that distinguishes it from bourbon: it undergoes a special method of filtration called the Lincoln County process. A Tennessee distiller named Alfred Eaton is credited with establishing the process in the 1820s, although some naysayers wonder if his name might have been connected to what was already a common practice.

Back in those days, Lincoln County was a much bigger territory. And in 1910, when Prohibition arrived early for Tennesseeans, more than 700 distilleries made whiskey using the Lincoln County process. Today, the only two distilleries in the state both use the process, but neither the Jack Daniel's nor the George Dickel distilleries are located in the current, much smaller version of Lincoln County.

The process—also known as charcoal mellowing or leaching—starts with sugar maple trees that are harvested during colder months, when they are low in sap, and then air-dried and

The process—also known as charcoal mellowing or leaching—starts with sugar maple trees that are harvested during colder months, when they are low in sap, and then air-dried and cut into boards.

cut into boards. At the distilleries, the boards are stacked in a lattice pattern to form "ricks," which are burned to make charcoal.

While men with hoses control the fire, the gaps in the ricks allow air to circulate through the wood when it is burned to make sure that charcoal, rather than ashes, will be the final result. After being broken into smallish pieces, the charcoal is piled into vats to a height of about eight to ten feet.

At both Tennessee distilleries, the new whiskey goes from the top of the vat to the bottom in about ten days—give or take a few days. (A wool blanket at the bottom keeps charcoal from coming out as well.) The whiskeys become lighter in the process and take on a certain sooty quality.

Dickel incorporates a couple of other variations. The vats are filled before they are allowed to drain to promote an even flow. And the vats are refrigerated, because a master distiller once liked the whiskeys better when they were filtered during winter months.

Among the Tennessee whiskeys produced these days, Jack Daniel's Old No. 7 Brand—the one with the black label—is one of the world's best-selling spirits. It is light in body but rambunctious in flavor. George Dickel No. 12 Superior Brand is a little fuller in body with a lush complexity. Both distilleries make other products as well, but these are the ones to try first.

Some distillers have gone to rather superstitious extremes to guard their yeast. Ova Haney, a master distiller at what is now known as the Four Roses Distillery, told an oral historian in 1985 about a sign in one facility's yeast room that said, "No Women Allowed." "There was the fear," Haney said, "that yeast in the presence of women having their period would . . . the yeast would die. . . . Like people used to say that, you know, a woman having her period can't make bread, because the yeast wouldn't rise. You know, it's carried from other old wives' tales."

In those days homegrown strains were called jug yeast, and they were started and maintained in actual jugs. Today things are quite different. "When we refer to 'jugs,' we're talking about copper vessels that are approximately 25 gallons," Jerry Dalton says. "This so-called jug is copper, and it has a valve and sits in a cradle—literally, a yeast cooler. We can rock its cradle to stir it up and draw off whatever volume of it we need."

Of course, Beam's operation dwarfs all other bourbon production. Most distillers maintain their working supplies of yeast—generated from the mother—in smaller vessels and use larger tubs, called donas, to produce enough working yeast for a batch of whiskey.

Sometimes hops are added to the yeast mash—as a preservative or as a flavor enhancer—and,

as a result, the yeast is considered to have been "soured." That should not be confused, but probably is, with the practice of adding lactic bacteria to yeast in order to increase acidity and influence flavor, which creates what is known as sour yeast mash.

Yeast goes into the fermenter with cooled mash and what is known as backset, liquid leftovers from the still after a batch of spirit has been made. Some—rather confusingly—call these leftovers setback. This ingredient is also—and this should sound familiar to those who study the labels of bourbon bottles—called sour mash.

The sour-mash process, which was developed by Dr. James Crow in the middle of the 19th century, has long been the standard operating procedure. In *The Book of Bourbon*, Gary Regan and Mardee Haidin Regan refer to sour mash as "whiskey DNA," something "to help get fermentation going on its own particular 'genetic' or 'family' path." David Pickerell, master distiller at Maker's Mark, says that backset "helps to create the proper environment for the yeast because it's acidic. Bacteria in general don't like acid, so they won't live in the fermenter, and the yeast don't mind it."

So the mash, yeast, and backset go into the fermenting tank, which traditionally was made of cypress but now is almost always made of stainless steel. Over the course of a few days, the liquid bubbles, then burbles, then splashes and foams up, then bubbles, then barely moves.

The movement of the liquid depends on the gas-producing action of the yeast, and the action in the fermenter calms when the yeast has done its job, leaving a liquid that has an alcohol content of 6 to 8 percent. This liquid has a new name: beer, or distiller's beer. But it doesn't taste quite like the stuff that comes in six-packs; for one thing, it doesn't have the hoppy bite of commercial brews, and for another, this beer is flat.

DISTILLATION

If you go to the places in Scotland where they make single-malt whisky, you can't help but be impressed by the beauty of the stills, with their gleaming copper, pot bellies, swan necks. Each represents a slight variation of the other—taller, fatter, shorter, thinner. Every one is a sculpture devoted to the art of distilling.

If you visit the places in Kentucky where they make bourbon—except for Woodford Reserve—you can't help but wonder which of the rather unimpressive pieces of equipment is the one that turns out the spirit.

The answer is the rather tall, unadorned cylinder. It goes by many names: column still (because it has the shape of a column), continu-

ous still (because, unlike a pot still, it produces spirits continuously and not in separate batches), Coffey still (after Aeneas Coffey, the 19th-century inventor who gets most of the credit for perfecting the device).

Inside this cylindrical column is a series of horizontal plates, perforated with tiny holes and set about 18 inches apart. Each plate has a tiny tube sticking up from it a few inches. Distiller's

Copper pot stills are common at Scottish distilleries, but only the Woodford Reserve Distillery uses them for bourbon in the States.

beer—with the grains—is pumped into the cylinder somewhere near the top.

Even though this thickened liquid does not come in at a gush—which might cause the grains to clog the holes and tubes—it accumulates on each plate faster than it can drip through the holes. When the level of the beer becomes high enough, it falls through the tube to the plate below.

Meanwhile, steam introduced from the bottom of the still rises and heats the dripping and falling beer. Because the boiling point of alcohol is lower than that of water, the alcohol content evaporates and rises, leaving behind nearly all of the water in the beer.

When these vapors reach the top of the column still, the first distillation is pretty much over. One of two devices is used for the next distillation: the thumper or the doubler.

The thumper is a closed tank partially filled with water. The vapors from the first distillation are channeled through it, and the remaining water content is left behind. This causes the water to churn and make a loud thumping noise, which explains how this piece of equipment got its name.

If a doubler is used, the vapors from the first distillation are condensed into liquid—called low wine or singlings—and then channeled into a smaller cylindrical still with a conical top. The

To be called bourbon, whiskey must age in charred barrels.

doubler is heated enough to vaporize the alcohol, but not the water, and when the spirit leaves the doubler it is condensed once more.

The vapors that come out of either a thumper or a doubler are called high wines or doublings. The thumper is cheaper to operate, but some bourbon people say it produces an earthier high wine, which may not be a problem for someone who wants a spirit with that quality.

The strength of the high wines will vary from one distillery to another, but bourbon cannot legally be distilled at higher than 160 proof. (Pure alcohol is 200 proof; half alcohol and half water is 100 proof.)

At Buffalo Trace, for example, low wines are about 120 proof, and the high wines—which can also be termed new-make spirit or white dog—are about 135 proof. "It's very hot and fiery in taste,"

The legal definition of bourbon says that the whiskey cannot be distilled higher than 160 proof (80 percent alcohol) and that it cannot be stronger than 125 proof (62.5 percent) when it is placed into barrels.

Elmer T. Lee says. "If you taste it at this point, you know why we barrel it and age it."

In contrast, the white dog at Wild Turkey, about 108 proof, is downright smooth and pleasantly grainy—just the way master distiller Jimmy Russell likes it. "The higher the proof you distill at, the less flavor you have," he says. "It's like a steak. If you cook it well done, there will be less flavor."

By law, bourbon cannot be barreled at more than 125 proof. White dog that's stronger than this is diluted with demineralized water. Some experts believe that a lower-proof whiskey will, over time, produce a more robust bourbon, while a higher proof will lead to a lighter whiskey.

Parker Beam of Heaven Hill disputes that assumption. "We've tried it at 105, 107, 110, 115,

117, 121—all different ranges of proof," he says, "and I really can't see any differences." There are financial reasons for barreling at the upper limit: by concentrating the strength of the spirit in a smaller volume of liquid, the distillery doesn't have to use as many barrels.

BARRELING

Yet another legal requirement for bourbon involves the kind of wood used for aging. Barrels must be made of oak, and they can be used only once.

There is a strong demand for used bourbon barrels—from whisky people in Scotland to tequila people in Mexico to rum people in Jamaica. Even blended American whiskeys can be aged in these vessels. But not bourbon.

The law doesn't require the barrels, which hold about 53 gallons, to be made specifically of American white oak, but this is the preferred choice among the bourbon industry. The tight grain of this wood keeps barrels from leaking.

Skilled workers known as coopers process the barrels in two main ways. At the Bluegrass Cooperage in Kentucky, staves are assembled and "toasted" with soft flames, transforming starches in the wood into sugar. Then the insides are charred by strong flames, caramelizing these sugars into what is called the red layer, just beneath

RYE

THE FINEST OF THE REFINED

At the turn of the 18th century, rye whiskey was the spirit of America. It came on strong as rum went into a decline, and there doesn't seem to be a simple explanation for the change in popular tastes.

Of course, it didn't hurt that George Washington became one of the leading producers of rye in the country after he retired to his estate at Mount Vernon, when he was persuaded by his overseer to pursue distillation.

The decline of rye in the 20th century is similarly cloaked in mystery. Some say that the whiskeys smuggled from Canada during Prohibition had an influence on taste buds, because they were lighter in body and flavor.

Others believe that the American distillation industry furthered the shift after Repeal, when they needed to bottle large quantities of whiskeys but had limited supplies of aged spirits in warehouses. To satisfy the born-again demand, distillers converted stronger straight whiskeys into softer and less challenging blends.

Legally, a straight rye whiskey must be made from a combination of grains that is made up of at least 51 percent rye, with the rest being corn and barley. Because rye produces a stronger and spicier spirit, a greater share of rye will lead to an even heavier whiskey with more zip. (As a rough comparison, think of the difference between corn bread and rye bread.)

The decline in sales of rye whiskey has, of course, meant that much less of it is produced. But certain companies—Buffalo Trace, Heaven Hill, Jim Beam, Wild Turkey—have been stalwart in their support of this great American spirit. Anchor, a small distillery in San Francisco, makes no whiskeys other than three ryes—and they are made with rye and rye alone.

Because rye produces a stronger and spicier spirit, a greater share of rye will lead to an even heavier whiskey with more zip.

Rye (the grain) will generally produce a more flavorful spirit, but rye—the whiskey—comes in a tantalizing variety of styles.

On the lighter end, Old Overholt is very easy to drink, while Wild Turkey and 100-proof Rittenhouse come with a considerable kick.

For the kind of rye character that resembles munching on a seed of rye, try Black Maple Hill or the Old Potrero whiskeys made by Anchor.

To prove the benefits of long and careful aging, Van Winkle Family Reserve shows the rich and full-bodied possibilities of rye whiskey, while Sazerac goes to a more subtle and elegant extreme.

Legally, straight rye whiskey must be made from a blend of grains comprising 51 percent rye (below), with the rest being corn and barley.

the blackened inside surface. At another major cooperage, Missouri's Independent Stave, the barrels go straight from construction to charring.

The levels of charring range from 1 (lightest) to 5 (darkest). All the major commercial distilleries use a level between 3.5 and 4.5. A number-4 char takes only about a minute of firing, and the difference between levels is just a few seconds of burn.

AGING

The barrel has a huge influence, but one that takes effect gradually over a period of years. Whiskey must be aged two years to be legally designated as bourbon. If it's been aged for less than four years, the length of time must be specified on the label.

Because bourbon drinkers prize a well-matured spirit, distillers often keep their whiskeys in barrels just past the four-year mark to avoid having a younger-age statement on the label. A significantly longer time in oak, on the other hand, will be proclaimed.

Aging is relatively fast paced in Kentucky thanks to the hot summers and the range of high and low temperatures, which sometimes vary widely in a single day. "When they talk about the weather in Kentucky," says Buffalo Trace's

Elmer T. Lee, "they say, 'If you don't like it, wait a few minutes. It'll change.' That's the sort of climate that's needed to make good bourbon."

In contrast, the uniformly cooler and damper climate in Scotland means that whiskies there take far longer to mature. Most Scottish single malts are aged for at least 12 years, which is quite old for a bourbon.

Shifts in temperature are important because the whiskey expands past the char layer and into the red layer when it gets hotter and then withdraws when it gets cooler. The red layer imparts flavors like vanilla and caramel to the whiskey, while the char acts as a kind of charcoal filter to remove bitterness.

Hotter weather pushes the spirit into the wood, where it extracts flavors—and all of its rich color. But there is also a reactive component to aging, as chemicals pulled out of the wood interact with chemicals in the spirit. For example, acetic acid from the wood and certain acids in the whiskey will come together to produce, among other things, compounds called esters. Chemical names aside, one of the by-products of this collaboration is a berrylike flavor and aroma.

While extracted flavors and aromas—vanilla and caramel—can be detected almost immediately after barreling, the reactive flavors and aromas—fruitiness, spiciness, floral accents—emerge very

slowly. Tannins, which are astringent compounds that contribute to the texture of the bourbon and provide a little bite, may not develop fully for six or eight years.

As time goes by, the strength of bourbon increases, whereas in Scotland the proof level of whisky goes down. No one has an exact explanation for this difference, although some believe that new barrels in Kentucky have open pores through which water can readily escape. In Scotland, where most of the barrels have been used before, those pores become somewhat blocked.

In both countries, however, some of the spirit is lost to evaporation, a portion known as the angel's share.

The microclimate of each warehouse, or "rickhouse," affects how the whiskey ages. Some distilleries heat these buildings in winter, so the

SOUTHERN
COMFORT

Not much is known about M. W. Heron beyond the fact that he invented Southern Comfort in 1874 because he received bad bourbon at his New Orleans bar.

Quality control wasn't quite as well developed then, and Heron couldn't count on spirits to deliver a consistent mix of flavors and aromas.

So he took matters into his hands, along with a few specific ingredients that he mixed into the bourbon. "When M. W. Heron tried to stabilize this whiskey, he picked ingredients that were indigenous to the surrounding area," says Lou Giglio, global brand ambassador for Southern Comfort. "To his whiskey, he added ripe orange, peaches, stone fruit like pitted cherries. He used lemon, lime, all the things that grew in abundance. Because New Orleans is a great port, he had access to the best cinnamon from Morocco, vanilla from Mexico."

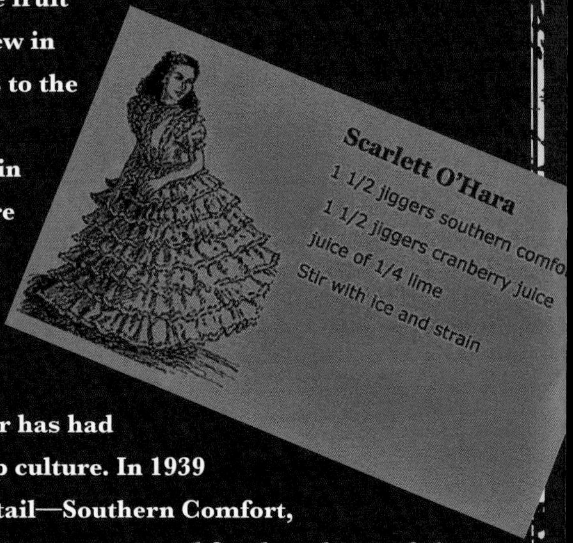

In 1889 Heron began to sell this blend in bottles that carried his personal signature and the motto "None genuine but mine." Fifteen years later, Southern Comfort won a gold medal at the St. Louis World's Fair.

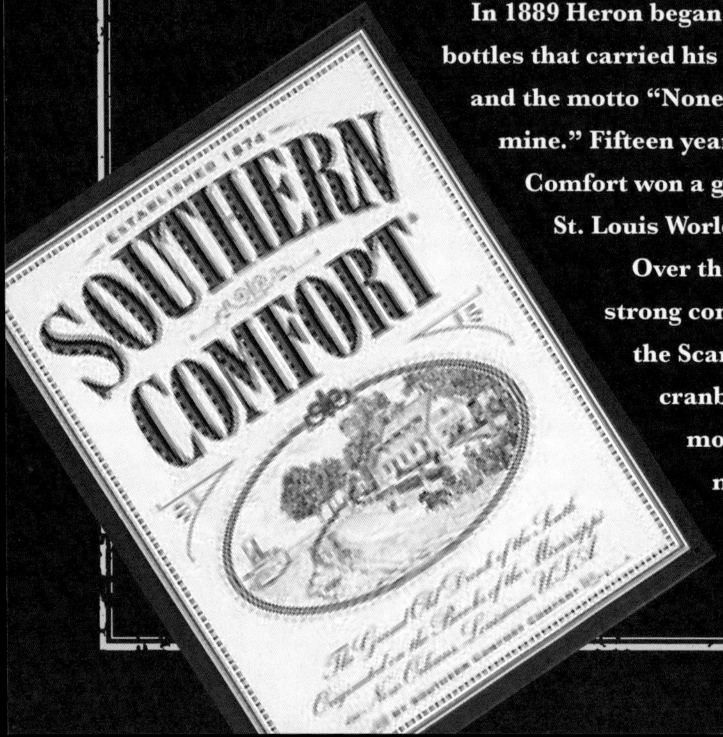

Over the years the liqueur has had strong connections with pop culture. In 1939 the Scarlett O'Hara cocktail—Southern Comfort, cranberry juice, and lime—was created for the release of the movie *Gone With the Wind*. About 30 years later, the spirit made a youthful comeback when rock singer Janis Joplin declared it her drink of choice.

Scarlett O'Hara
1 1/2 jiggers southern comfo
1 1/2 jiggers cranberry juice
juice of 1/4 lime
Stir with ice and strain

SOUTHERN COMFORT
ESTABLISHED 1874

Today the recipe for Southern Comfort includes more than 30 ingredients, but none of them is bourbon. A rum distillate is blended with other ingredients in St. Croix and then shipped in concentrated form to three places in the world (Kentucky, Ireland, and South Africa), where it is brought to full strength. Aside from the fact that Heron invented Southern Comfort in New Orleans and spent some time in St. Louis, where he is buried, the inventive barman's life is a mystery. At one point Brown-Forman—the company that owns the brand—offered a $10,000 reward to anyone who could produce a verifiable photograph of Heron. The money was never claimed.

The Scarlett O'Hara cocktail—Southern Comfort, cranberry juice, and lime—was created for the release of the movie Gone With the Wind. *About 30 years later, the spirit made a youthful comeback when rock singer Janis Joplin declared it her drink of choice.*

bourbon extracts more throughout the year and develops its extracted qualities at a faster pace.

Heating has been more common for facilities located in cities, where the rickhouses are usually built of brick, than for distilleries in smaller towns or out in the country, where the warehouses are metal clad.

Buffalo Trace, located in the city of Frankfort, uses heat to keep its warehouses at around 50 degrees during colder weather. "You can achieve about a six-year equivalent of aging at four years," Elmer T. Lee says, "or at the end of six years you can achieve the equivalent of about eight years of aging in an unheated warehouse."

Brown-Forman goes even farther. During colder weather, the distillery puts its warehouses in Louisville and Versailles through hot-and-cold cycles of about two weeks in duration. All the floors are heated to 90 degrees; then the windows are opened so that the warehouse cools to about 75 degrees. "We can get 11 or 12 cycles during the wintertime," Chris Morris says.

Some distillers will have none of this. Jimmy Russell of Wild Turkey prefers what he calls the "natural aging" of his unheated warehouses in the country around Lawrenceburg. "Our storage buildings are open when the temperature is in the 70s and on up, and we shut them back down when the temperature gets lower," he says. "We want the

change of seasons. I like to say that our warehouses are climate controlled—we open them in the summertime, and we close them in the wintertime."

Most of the warehouses in Kentucky are several stories tall, and when the windows are open, a chimney effect increases the highly desirable flow of air up and around the barrels. The upward movement, caused by the rising of hotter air, means that the upper floors of a warehouse will be hotter than the lower reaches. That difference can be as large as 40 degrees or more.

Over time, the temperature differences among floors cause individual barrels to mature at different rates. To create a more uniform whiskey, a few distilleries—Maker's Mark to the greatest extent—"rotate" barrels from higher floors to lower.

"The stuff at the very top is cooking on high," David Pickerell says, "and the stuff at the bottom is on simmer." At Maker's Mark, barrels enter on high, where warmer conditions spur extraction. Eventually barrels move below for a more reactive phase. Somewhere between five years, nine months, and seven years, the barrel is ready to roll to the bottling line.

Many distilleries—Beam, for example—keep all their barrels in place until time for dumping. To achieve uniformity, barrels with different characteristics are combined to create the desired flavor profile. With an inventory of barrels that numbers in the hundreds of thousands, Beam has a lot to choose from.

Four Roses, on the other hand, doesn't need to rotate, because all of its warehouses are single-story structures. "The temperature differential in our warehouses is a maximum of eight degrees," master distiller Jim Rutledge says. "It's easier to come up with our finished bourbons because our production is so consistent."

During the aging process, master distillers monitor what is going on inside the barrels. They know from experience that the sweet spot of a given warehouse lies in the very middle—in the middle of the floor, on the floors that are in the middle of the building.

Some designate this area the "center cut," and most of the premium bourbons are aged there, in what the industry calls honey barrels. Booker's, the highest of the high-end whiskeys in Beam's Small Batch Collection, comes from the middle floors—six, seven, and eight—of a warehouse that former master distiller Jerry Dalton declines to identify.

While steel and copper fermentation vessels have made their way into production lines,
many bourbons are still placed in barrels so they may capture more complex flavors from the charred-oak interiors.

MOONSHINE

*I*t goes by many names: skull cracker, bush whiskey, ruckus juice, mule kick, hillbilly pop, panther's breath, tiger's sweat, happy sally, blue john, old horsey, block and tackler, white lightning. But the oldest term is the one folks know best: moonshine.

Originally, back in Scotland or Ireland (both places claim to be where whiskey got its start), underground distillation was often just that. Not only did people make the stuff by moonlight in pits and caves, they would move the spirit in the middle of the night and, even more undetectably, during nasty storms. In much the same way that their descendants would one day sneak around the backwoods of the southeast United States, these Scottish and Irish bootleggers stuck to the rugged terrain and rough pathways where officials feared to tread.

The major issue back then—as now—was taxes. Royalty wanted money, to fight wars or to pay for the luxuries of court life. And distillers did their best to avoid paying these levies.

Some of these moonshiners, like their Kentucky kin a few times removed, would eventually go legit. One of the great whisky houses of Scotland, The Glenlivet, has its roots in a still that was

hidden in the hills near the River Spey. The man who founded the company, George Smith, was the first to get a proper license in 1824, when the Crown made it legal to distill.

When, near the turn of the 18th century, the fledging American republic decided to raise money by taxing distillation, the Scotch-Irish led the first armed insurgency against the United States. The Whiskey Rebellion may have given the government second thoughts

Prohibition changed the character of the people who made moonshine. The national ban created an enormous demand, thus leading to a more organized kind of criminal activity.

(and caused revenue agents to collect levies with a certain regard for self-preservation), but taxes against booze would come and go throughout the 19th century. Moonshine activity would rise and fall in direct response.

And then came Prohibition. In her book *Moonshine: Its History and Folklore,* Esther Kellner writes, "Moonshiners had reason to look upon the Temperance workers as angels unaware, for the greatest good fortune that could come to any industry, high or low, came to them when the country went dry in 1919. Backwoods grog, which had been selling for $2 a gallon and less, now brought $22 a gallon, with no questions asked. The Temperance workers had won the battle and lost the war."

Prohibition also changed the character of the people who made this whiskey. Before 1919 most of the moonshine was sold in the communities where it was produced. But the national ban created an enormous demand, which meant distribution to other areas of the country, thus leading to a more organized kind of criminal activity. Even after Repeal some of these larger, mobbed-up enterprises continued. Recent years have seen a few major cases, including one against distillers in North Carolina who were shipping to unlicensed clubs along the Eastern Seaboard.

Far more common, however, are smaller operators who may be the sons—and sons of sons— of folks who have made moonshine a family business. For instance, a number of moonshiners went from racing revenuers to challenging stock-car drivers in the early days of NASCAR. Junior Johnson won the Daytona 500 in 1960, just a few years after serving 11 months in jail for roaring down country roads with hooch made by his family. Asked to compare his experience on the NASCAR circuit to that of the polished competitors of today, Johnson told a reporter in 2005, "I don't think Jeff Gordon has the backbone to run moonshine. He'd probably have a heart attack the first time a red light come on."

The taste of moonshine hasn't changed that much over the years. Some people toss in a little grain for flavor, but a lot of the stuff is made from granulated sugar, gets bottled right away, and causes a commotion as it travels through your innards. Nevertheless, folks with a taste for white lightning—preferring the thunder it produces between the ears—wouldn't let any other "likker" past their lips.

Distillers do everything they can to achieve consistency. They try to mash and ferment and distill and age their whiskeys in exactly the same way, day in and day out, so customers will experience the same aromas and flavors every time they pick up a fresh bottle of an old favorite.

Nevertheless, whiskeys come out of the barrels with easily detectable differences. "I once evaluated 1,200 barrels over a six-month period," Jerry Dalton says, "and I'll tell you, barrels sitting side by side in a warehouse on the same floor, barreled on the same day from the same cistern tank in the distillery, are still as individual as fingerprints."

Even if barrels show a family resemblance, that's not good enough. Distillers sometimes mingle whiskeys from several hundreds of barrels for their less expensive brands.

This process involves "blending," but that can be a loaded term in distilling. "Blended whiskeys," in the American industry, refers to those products that combine straight whiskeys with other whiskeys or neutral-grain spirits or both.

The same holds true, by the way, in Scotland. A single-malt Scotch, for example, is a mingling of whiskies from a single malt distillery, such as The Macallan—unless the bottling is specifically called a single-barrel product. A blended Scotch, such as Chivas Regal, is a combination of malt whiskies made in pot stills from individual distilleries, and grain whiskies made elsewhere with column stills.

When Jim Beam created its Small Batch Bourbon Collection in 1992, its use of the term *small* was valid in comparison to its usual huge batch size. Knob Creek, Basil Hayden's, and Baker's are put together in relatively small batches of 200 to 400 barrels.

Other companies, which may be run by a handful of people who don't do their own distilling, often produce high-quality bourbon in batches that are minuscule by comparison to Beam—as few as 15 barrels. But even Maker's Mark, produced all year round and widely distributed, has a small-batch scale. It's bottled in batches of about 20 barrels.

Single-barrel bourbons, even from the same brand, are meant to be different—but not too different. For these, one barrel is dumped and bottled. That's followed by another single barrel, and then another, and so on. While the master distiller may choose barrels that have a resemblance to earlier single-barrel bottlings, no mingling is involved.

Before bourbon goes into bottles it is filtered, essentially for appearances. If not, the whiskey might take on a cloudy appearance when it is

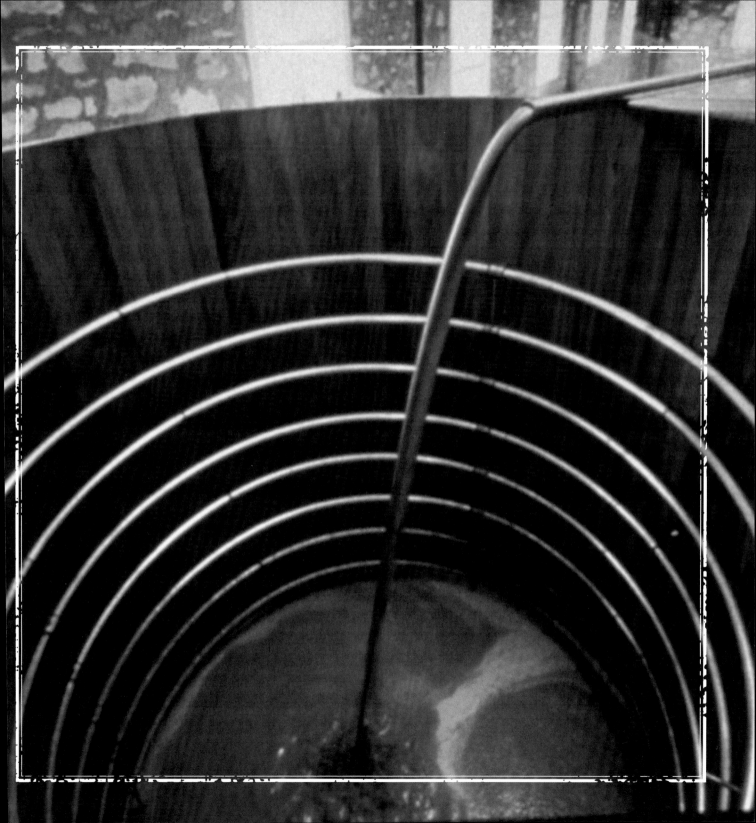

cold. Filtration occurs either at room temperature or when chilled. Booker's is the only widely available bourbon that is not filtered this way.

When distillers like the ones quoted above talk about the way they make bourbon—from the milling of grain to the filling of bottles—it becomes clear just how their craft has evolved slowly over time, like a kind of alcohol folk art.

Many of the practices that are now common were the result of happy accidents, or what David Pickerell of Maker's Mark calls "formalized serendipity." One distiller tried something and it worked, so he kept doing it. Others tried it and it worked, so it became a standard practice.

Part of bourbon's charm comes from the way it connects back in time with the people who have made it and the people who have drunk it. It is now, and has been for more than 200 years, an icon of American culture. And it tastes mighty fine on the rocks.

When filled with about 53 gallons of bourbon, barrels weigh about 550 pounds,
so they are often rolled out to trucks to be transported.

When distillers talk about the way they make bourbon—from the milling of grain to the filling of bottles—it becomes clear how their craft has evolved slowly over time, like a kind of alcohol folk art.

CHAPTER TWO

Rendering of the old Heaven Hill distillery in Bardstown, which was destroyed in a November 1996 fire.

COURTING BOURBON
A Suitor's Tutorial

*Bourbon has a history so American that the whiskey
should come not only in red (as in "red likker") but also in white and blue.*

The tale can be told, in textbook style, as a series of sweeping changes that parallel the development of the United States, moving from the original Eastern colonies to the West and from agrarian roots to industrialized dominance.

The tale can also be told through the determination (or desperation), the stubbornness (or ignorance), and the resourcefulness (or feloniousness) of individuals who pursued their entrepreneurial instincts with the intensity—and tang—of "white lightning."

When you pick up a bottle of bourbon, you touch a little bit of this history. Look at the label, and you'll see the words "straight bourbon whiskey" (or "whisky," for those who use the spelling common in England, Scotland, and Canada). That phrase represents a turning point: the Pure Food and Drug Bill, passed by Congress on June 30, 1906, which essentially defined bourbon as we know it today.

In the 21st century, the legal definition of "straight" (versus plain) bourbon is well established. It must be made primarily from corn, meaning that at least 51 percent of the mix of grains must be corn. It must be distilled to no more than 160 proof and put into barrels at no more than 125 proof. It must spend a minimum of two years in those barrels, which have been charred on the inside and which can be used only once.

Four hundred years ago, when distillation got under way in the American colonies, there were no standards—just a well-developed taste for malt whisky (made with barley) that came with immigrants out of Scotland and Ireland. Although the colonists brought beer and hard alcohol across the Atlantic with them, these stocks were eventually drained.

But when the colonists got ready to reproduce their favorite drinks, some accommodations had to be made. The New World had apples, which could be made into cider and applejack, and other fruit that could be made into brandy, but no barley, the key ingredient for the whisky they knew from home.

So the story of bourbon begins with the grain that the first immigrants from England called "Indian corn" because it was a plant as native to the land as the people who greeted these new arrivals fresh off the boat. Some colonists used corn to make beer that was not entirely to their liking, and others transformed this fermented beverage into whiskey by distilling it.

Colonial distillation of corn and rye and wheat became so popular that it caused grain shortages during the Revolutionary War, leading to a ban on the "distilling of unreasonable Quantities of Wheat and other Grain into Whisky." Those were the words of George Washington— first in war, first in peace, and first in American distilling. After retiring to his estate at Mount Vernon, Washington became one of the leading whiskey producers in the country.

In the colonies and in the newborn United States, however, the spirit of choice was rum. Its production was tied to the scurrilous phenomenon known as "triangle trade." West Africans were kidnapped and shipped to the Caribbean, where some were traded for sugarcane and molasses (the first leg of the triangle). Slaves, sugarcane, and molasses were brought to New England, where

Moonshiners could be found everywhere in the late 18th century after the taxation of liquor was first established, but this 1867 illustration is labeled as the "Southern Mode of Making Whisky."

the cane and molasses were made into rum (the second), and the finished product was sent to West Africa, where it was exchanged for more slaves (the third).

Around 1800, as major trading nations began to ban slavery and restrict the trade of human bodies—importation of slaves to the United States became illegal in 1808—Americans were turning to whiskey. It had become so prominent by 1794 that a new tax on whiskey spurred an armed insurrection in western Pennsylvania. The Whiskey Rebellion was short lived, but it established a tradition of resistance among small distillers that exists today with the continued making of moonshine in rural areas, mostly in the South.

By the turn of the 19th century, whiskeymaking in the Ohio River Valley was fairly common, particularly in what is now Kentucky. Land was granted to those who stopped to put down roots (mostly corn, but also rye) and put up buildings (mostly homes, but mills and stillhouses as well). Water in the area was ideal for whiskey production because so much of it flowed through limestone springs, which gave it just the right chemical balance. And forests provided a supply of wood that could be used to make staves for barrels.

No one knows who was the first to distill whiskey in Kentucky, and there's a very good reason why the mystery remains unsolved: way too

Horsepower in the form of trucks now transports bourbon around the distillery grounds, but even as the middle of the 20th century was approaching, companies relied upon mule power.

many suspects. In the invaluable history *Kentucky Bourbon: The Early Years of Whiskeymaking*, Henry Crowgey writes, "The distillation of liquor or brandy occupied the same place in their lives as did the making of soap, the grinding of grain in a rude hand mill, or the tanning of animal pelts."

If the honor went to the most colorful distiller rather than the first one, two men would be strong candidates: Rev. Elijah Craig and Evan Williams, both of whom have modern-day whiskeys named after them. Craig was jailed in Virginia for controversial preaching activities before moving near what is now Georgetown, Kentucky,

ABRAHAM
LINCOLN

Without bourbon, our 16th president might never have been called "Honest Abe." It all has to do with a general store in New Salem, Illinois, that Abraham Lincoln co-owned with William F. Berry for about a year, starting in 1832.

In his autobiography, writing about himself as if describing someone else, Lincoln recalls, "He studied what he should do—thought of learning the blacksmith trade—thought of trying to study law—rather thought he could not succeed at that without a better education. Before long, strangely enough, a man offered to sell, and did sell, to Abraham and another as poor as himself, an old stock of goods, upon credit. They opened as merchants; and he says that was the store."

During its brief run, the store sold and bartered such goods as eggs, bacon, honey, beeswax, muslin, calico, firearms—and whiskey. At first, the liquor was sold in larger quantities for consumption outside the store, but then they applied for a license to sell drinks on the premises. Although the names of both Lincoln and Berry appear on the license, granted on March 6, 1833, Lincoln's signature is considered a forgery, probably by Berry.

Not only did this extra service not save the business, but it is widely believed that Berry himself was a major consumer of the store's whiskey stocks. In 1835 Berry died, and Lincoln assumed all of his partner's financial liabilities, a total debt of about $1,100—a rather staggering amount for a man of Lincoln's limited means.

Later he would lightheartedly refer to this sum as "the national debt." And the payment of this obligation, although it was not directly his, became the cornerstone of the future president's reputation for dependability and honesty.

Not much is known about Lincoln's personal consumption of liquor. Some vague claims have circulated that his father, Thomas Lincoln, may have worked in a distillery near Knob Creek, the site of young Abe's second childhood home.

Benjamin P. Thomas, in his biography of Abraham Lincoln, speculates that Lincoln must have sampled spirits a little as he grew older, since he once remarked that liquor made him feel "flabby and undone." He would have had ready access, and not just at the general store. Lincoln spoke of working "the latter part of one winter in a little stillhouse up at the head of a hollow."

While he might not have enjoyed liquor, Lincoln seemed to tolerate it. In 1842 his address to the Springfield Washington Temperance Society took issue with harsher attitudes toward alcohol, advocating reason and persuasion for those who wanted to control liquor consumption.

On the presidential campaign trail in 1858, Lincoln used humor to counter a charge from his opponent, Stephen A. Douglas, that he must have encouraged the use of whiskey because he sold it at the New Salem store. "The difference between Judge Douglas and myself is just this," Lincoln said, "that while I was behind the bar, he was in front of it."

The store sold and bartered such goods as eggs, bacon, honey, beeswax, muslin, calico, firearms—and whiskey.

to start a farm, mill, and distillery. Williams, who made whiskey in Louisville along the Ohio River, was charged with distilling without a license and was considered a nuisance for his sloppy handling of water and leftover grain—not to mention his habit of showing up drunk at town meetings.

The first Kentucky whiskey—no matter who made it—would not have resembled the bourbon we drink today. It may have been grain whiskey, made predominantly or entirely with corn, but it wasn't aged in charred oak barrels, so it would have lacked the reddish-brown color we now expect. And nearly all of it would have gone quickly from the maker to the drinker, with maybe a brief stop at a store or a tavern. Whether taken directly from a jug or dispensed into a glass, this whiskey would have packed an extra wallop.

As the 19th century unfolded, some of the production techniques that are now standard—as well as the term *bourbon*—came into common use. The aging of whiskey seems to have developed along two different tracks, both related to commercial forces. Those distillers who produced more whiskey than they could sell would have kept the extra in barrels for a significant amount of time, causing a notable difference in flavor and texture.

When distillers began to ship whiskey downriver—after the course of the Mississippi River south to New Orleans passed into Ameri-

can control early in the 19th century—the trip would take a few months, and the spirit would be sold at various stops along the way. This allowed boatmen to observe how time in the barrel made certain improvements and how their customers enjoyed the difference.

The shipping of whiskey down the Mississippi may be the origin of the name *bourbon*, although this is another mystery with very few clues. As the legend goes, people who bought this stuff downriver would refer to it as "whiskey from Bourbon," alluding to Bourbon County in Kentucky, a territory much larger than the county now covers. The first known advertisement to mention "bourbon whiskey" appeared in June of 1821, and within two decades the term was common.

Advertisements from the period also help to narrow the time frame when aging first took

As this 1870 ad for Old Crow demonstrates, the twinning of liquor ads and the female form has a long, somewhat lurid history.

place in charred barrels, although yet again there are no definitive answers. Distillers did not begin using the color of their products as a selling point until about 1820, and that's significant because those deep hues come from barrels that have been charred. So, it's safe to assume that charring started shortly before this time. But why would the barrels have been fired up? Probably because all manner of merchandise got sent in them, leaving plenty of barrels for reuse, but only after distillers burned the insides to keep the influence of previous contents from introducing nasty flavors and aromas.

One other technique developed during the second quarter of the 19th century helped to create bourbon as we know it. Dr. James Crow perfected the use of residue from an earlier batch of whiskey—"sour mash"—to create a consistent product with each new batch. The method was adopted throughout the bourbon industry.

Although Crow made bourbon for only about 20 years, from 1840 until his death in 1856, his whiskey became very popular. Ulysses S. Grant, in particular, favored Old Crow. He might have liked it a little too much, since his reputation as a heavy drinker hampered his career—in the eyes of all but President Abraham Lincoln, who said that if Grant's brand "made fighting generals like Grant, I should like to get some of it for distribution."

The restrictions of Prohibition spawned a sophisticated, widespread black market in liquor, complete with well-developed networks of distribution, as this undated photo of a raided warehouse shows.

As bourbon gained in popularity in the years leading up to the Civil War, a number of businessmen were able to profit from differing notions of what the whiskey actually was. In their definitive survey, *The Book of Bourbon and Other Fine American Whiskeys*, Gary Regan and Mardee Haidin Regan tell of middlemen who blended bourbons from different producers into their own distinctive products. Others took whiskey in bulk and processed it to remove impurities. Then there were "scalawags," as the Regans put it, who "blended small amounts of straight whiskey with huge quantities of flavorless neutral grain spirits

Some of the equipment used to make illegal spirits during Prohibition was crude, as seen in this 1921 photo, and the hooch was carried in everything from Mason jars to easily concealed flasks (right).

and a few flavorings, then sold their product as 'straight whiskey.' "

A new type of still perfected just before the Civil War by an Irishman named Aeneas Coffey made such "creative" marketing even easier. Known variously as the Coffey still, the patent still, and the continuous still, this device could generate large amounts of neutral grain spirits. And it could also turn out bourbon more quickly and more economically than the pot still, although the whiskeys it produced did not always have the same robust character as those from a pot still.

In the years leading up to the turn of the 20th century, innovations in the glass industry allowed mass production of bottles with small necks. Distillers were now able to package their products for widespread sale to consumers rather than using retailers to transfer whiskey from barrels to smaller

containers. This made it possible to develop brands of whiskey that could be marketed on a regional or national basis.

In 1906 the definition of bourbon got some much-needed clarity after an intense debate in Congress. Both the people who sold their whiskey uncut and the people who blended it with neutral grain spirits staked claims to being "pure," but the Pure Food and Drug Act distinguished between the two types by focusing on the ways in which they were made—"straight" (or uncut) versus "blended."

The considerable growth of operating costs caused the number of bourbon distillers to shrink over time, but the onset of Prohibition in January 1920 finally killed most of the industry. While a few distilleries were allowed to make and store whiskey for medicinal purposes after the 18th Amendment to the Constitution went into effect, others were dismantled. Of the 17 plants making whiskey before Prohibition, only 7 were operating in the years after it ended on December 20, 1933.

In his history of the Jim Beam brand, *American Still Life*, F. Paul Pacult describes severe financial difficulties suffered by Beam himself, who turned unsuccessfully to other ventures after he had to abandon the bourbon business. While shopping for groceries in the late 1920s, Beam had to return some items to shelves because he had only $5 in cash. "The Beams were broke," said one eyewitness. Of course, the Jim Beam brand would make

BEAM
FAMILY TREE

JACOB BEAM

DAVID BEAM

JOSEPH M. BEAM

MINOR CASE BEAM
M.C. BEAM
DISTILLERY

JOSEPH L. "MR. JOE" BEAM
STITZEL-WELLER DISTILLERY AND OLD HEAVEN HILL SPRINGS DISTILLERY

GUY

ELMO
MAKER'S MARK
DISTILLERY

ROY
FRANKFORT
DISTILLERY

WILMER
TAYLOR & WILLIAMS
DISTILLERY

DESMOND
FRANKFORT DISTILLERY AND
MASTER DISTILLER AT
OLD KENNEBEC DISTILLERY

EVERETT
MASTER DISTILLER
MICHTER'S DISTILLERY

OTIS

HARRY
MASTER DISTILLER
OLD HEAVEN HILL SPRINGS
DISTILLERY

WALTER

JACK
BARTON
DISTILLERY

CHARLES
SEAGRAM'S FOUR ROSES
DISTILLERY

JACK
TAYLOR & WILLIAMS
DISTILLERY

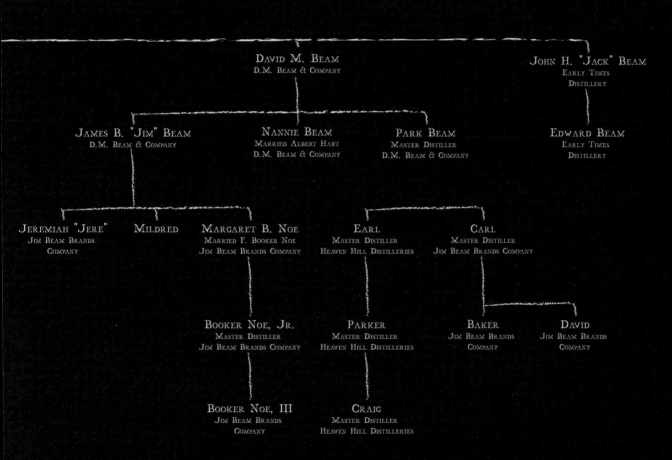

DAVID M. BEAM
D.M. BEAM & COMPANY

JOHN H. "JACK" BEAM
EARLY TIMES
DISTILLERY

JAMES B. "JIM" BEAM
D.M. BEAM & COMPANY

NANNIE BEAM
MARRIED ALBERT HART
D.M. BEAM & COMPANY

PARK BEAM
MASTER DISTILLER
D.M. BEAM & COMPANY

EDWARD BEAM
EARLY TIMES
DISTILLERY

JEREMIAH "JERE"
JIM BEAM BRANDS
COMPANY

MILDRED

MARGARET B. NOE
MARRIED F. BOOKER NOE
JIM BEAM BRANDS COMPANY

EARL
MASTER DISTILLER
HEAVEN HILL DISTILLERIES

CARL
MASTER DISTILLER
JIM BEAM BRANDS COMPANY

BOOKER NOE, JR.
MASTER DISTILLER
JIM BEAM BRANDS COMPANY

PARKER
MASTER DISTILLER
HEAVEN HILL DISTILLERIES

BAKER
JIM BEAM BRANDS
COMPANY

DAVID
JIM BEAM BRANDS
COMPANY

BOOKER NOE, III
JIM BEAM BRANDS
COMPANY

CRAIG
MASTER DISTILLER
HEAVEN HILL DISTILLERIES

an incredible comeback after Repeal, eventually becoming the best-selling bourbon in the world.

Not only did Prohibition change the nature of the bourbon business, it profoundly changed the American taste for alcohol. During the 13 years that the country was allegedly dry, the spirit most readily available for the widespread flouting of the law was cheap gin, which was much lighter in body and flavor than bourbon. And distillers reinforced this preference after Repeal, stretching the limited supply of bourbon by channeling much of it into lighter blended whiskeys.

From the late 1930s to the early 1990s the story of bourbon is dominated by business developments that parallel those in the larger world of commerce. Mergers and acquisitions reduced the number of distillers over time, and some companies expanded from bourbon into additional spirits and, in some cases, different types of businesses entirely. Other distilling companies were taken over by foreign investors.

The dawning of the 21st century brought an old-fashioned twist to the bourbon industry. The shift has been partly attributed, strangely enough, to the crackdown on drunk driving. Americans began to drink less but drink better. That trend has taken bourbon back to the good old days, at least when it comes to full-flavored whiskey being put in bottles. And that's worth celebrating with a toast to the fine folks who've made bourbon what it is—from Rev. Elijah Craig to James E. Crow to Jim Beam to the master distillers of today.

Beam family portrait.

CHAPTER THREE

Fabled copper pots used by Labrot & Graham to distill bourbon in Versailles, Kentucky

Refinement and Refiners

Once upon a time—1919, to be precise—
it was easy to find a bourbon distillery in Kentucky.

Before Prohibition went into effect that year, 183 distilleries were operating in the commonwealth, according to Sam K. Cecil, a former master distiller at Maker's Mark and author of *The Evolution of the Bourbon Whiskey Industry in Kentucky.* There were 23 in Nelson County alone.

Now only ten remain in the whole state, operated by eight companies, and they are responsible for virtually all of the bourbon produced in the entire United States.

The process of going from the big number to the small number has not been easy to follow. Distilleries have been sold, resold, resold, and so on—sometimes for the brands they controlled, sometimes for the stocks of whiskey in their warehouses, sometimes for the warehouses themselves, and sometimes for other reasons too numerous to mention.

This chapter offers historical sketches of major straight-bourbon producers, who have survived the ups and downs of the whiskey business as well as the challenges of consolidation and globalization that have affected all American companies. Microdistillers have not been included because none have yet to produce straight bourbon whiskey at the time of this writing.

In addition, this section includes, at shorter length, those companies that sell high-end whiskey distilled by others and, in some cases, aged by others as well. These businesses can be described by various names: rectifiers, blenders, bottlers, resellers.

Some of these companies even call themselves distilleries, although they are distillers only in name. Very few of them are forthcoming about their operations, preferring not to reveal the source (or sources) of their whiskeys. (Yet do not judge their secrecy as an indication of poor quality. They often produce bourbon of the highest order.)

BARTON DISTILLERY
Bardstown, Kentucky

Y ou can trace the lineage of this company back to an extraordinary bit of risqué marketing. The company was Mattingly & Moore, formed in 1877 by the team of J. G. Mattingly and Tom Moore. The label for their Belle of Nelson bourbon featured a bevy of naked women in what seems to be a harem—at least that explanation would account for the vaguely Middle Eastern décor and the man who appears to be carrying a hookah.

In his book *Bluegrass, Belles, and Bourbon* Harry Harrison Kroll comments upon this rather bold and exotic approach:

Anybody who has bent an elbow at the smelly polish of an old saloon bar, with its long mirror reflecting the puffed faces of the customers staring at the voluptuous nude reclining overhead, with her massive bosoms and bovian-shaped hips and that Mona Lisa smile that looked like a whore trying to make up her mind to lure a farm lad, without the grace even of a fig leaf . . . knows how closely associated are women and sex and alcoholic beverages.

Despite the marketing savvy of the team, Mattingly and Moore went their separate ways after four years. In 1889 Moore moved on to his own distillery on the present site of Barton's operation, and he did well up until the start of Prohibition. (Barton sells a brand that Moore named for himself, and another, Mattingly & Moore, that dates back to their short-lived partnership.)

The property was essentially gutted in 1919. A laundry operated on the premises until after Repeal in 1934, when Moore's son, Con, built a new distilling plant. This company did not prosper, and Oscar Getz took it over in 1944. During World War II the distillery was used to make high-proof industrial alcohol, and afterwards it returned to the production of bourbon.

Getz, who renamed the company Barton, was a devoted collector of equipment, bottles, and artifacts related to whiskey. After his death in

The basic ingredient in bourbon is corn, as the law requires that it make up at least 51 percent of the grain in any recipe. Most of the corn used is grown in Kentucky and nearby states.

1982 these materials, which had been on display at the distillery, became the Oscar Getz Museum of Whiskey History in Bardstown.

Canandaigua Wine bought the distillery in 1993 and continues to run it. This company, now called Constellation Brands, is the largest wine seller in the world, with such brands as Robert Mondavi, Almaden, Inglenook, Taylor, and Paul Masson.

Barton bourbons include: Ridgemont Reserve 1792, Barclay's, Colonel Lee, Kentucky Gentleman, Kentucky Tavern, Ten High, Tom Moore, Very Old Barton

Other Barton brands include: Black Velvet Canadian whisky, Speyburn Single Malt Scottish whisky, Fleischmann's vodka and gin, Monte Alban Mezcal, Corona beer, St. Pauli Girl beer, Negra Modelo beer, Tsingtao beer

JAMES B. BEAM DISTILLING COMPANY
Clermont, Kentucky, & Boston, Kentucky

Jim Beam bourbon is made by just one branch of the most illustrious family in American distilling. The founding father of this part of the clan, according to F. Paul Pacult's Beam history, *American Still Life*, was born between 1760 and 1765 in Pennsylvania as Johannes Jacob Boehm.

By the time of the first Kentucky census in 1790, however, he was going by the name of Jacob Beam. And by 1795 he had sold his first whiskey while working a farm and a mill, as well as a distillery, on his property along Hardin Creek.

Tending the stills at Labrot & Graham, Versailles, Kentucky

A special section of a Nelson County newspaper published in 1896 describes the establishment of the Beam distilling enterprise like this:

Away back in the last century, when Nelson County was among the first settled in the state, Jacob Beam, a young man of sterling worth and integrity, located in this county. He at once began the manufacture of whisky. There was very little profit in the business then, but it was suitable to the young man's inclinations, as it was about the only medicine known to the early settlers and he believed by giving it especial attention, as a business, some good would in the future, when the country became more densely populated, result from its manufacture.

These instincts proved correct. And Jacob Beam passed along his combination of business sense and whiskey sense to his tenth child, David, who took over the operation in 1820. It was known then as the Old Tub Distillery, and its success continued after one of David's three sons, David M., assumed control in 1853. (His brothers, Joseph M. and John H. ["Jack"], would spawn distillers as well, but for other companies.)

The next handoff, nearly 40 years later, was one of the pivotal moments in American distilling. In 1892 James Beauregard Beam, son of David M., began to run the company alongside Albert

J. Hall, son-in-law of David M. His nickname was Jim, and his name—Jim Beam—would one day go on the label and become synonymous around the world with bourbon itself.

But for the time being, the business—now known as the Beam and Hart Old Tub Distillery—was building a major reputation. And another twig off the family tree came on board: Jim Beam's son T. Jeremiah Beam.

Prohibition brought the business to a complete stop. Although Jim Beam was a wizard at making money in distilling, he had no choice but to try other industries. Ventures in mining and citrus farming failed, and his money was almost gone.

The repeal of Prohibition in 1933 set the stage for an astonishing comeback. Jim Beam's whiskey instincts, like those of his grandfather Jacob, were razor sharp. And he knew that great profits could quickly be made in bourbon after Repeal because of the gap between supply (understandably low) and demand (newly ravenous).

So Jim Beam charged back into the distilling business at the age of 69, telling T. Jeremiah and other family members, "Boys, time for us to get back to work." He raised money from three Chicago investors, who would own the company while the Beams ran it.

Together they built a new distillery over the course of 120 days in the fall of 1934. It was located near Clermont, Kentucky, on the site of a quarry that Jim Beam had purchased during Prohibition.

Because the family no longer owned the rights to the brand name Old Tub, the company chose to name its new brand after the head of the clan: Col. James B. Beam. (It was later shortened to Jim Beam.)

On the occasion of an open house for the company in 1935, Beam was asked what his yield of whiskey might be in the new facility. He replied, "I am not interested, sir, in how much, but how good a whiskey I can get out of a bushel."

While the distilling industry was slow to recover from Prohibition, and the need to produce industrial alcohol during World War II took away from bourbon making, the postwar period became a boom time for bourbon in general and Beam in particular.

Ownership of the company was consolidated in 1941, with one of the three partners, Phillip Blum, buying out the other two. But the Beam family continued to run the distillery and make whiskey in a very profitable fashion.

They were so profitable, in fact, that the Beam company outgrew its Clermont distillery. In 1953 the company revitalized a dormant distillery near Boston, Kentucky, to create a second production facility. Frederick Booker Noe II, a nephew of T. Jeremiah Beam and grandson of Jim Beam,

was put in charge. He would become a modern legend in bourbon.

The company's ownership shifted at the end of December 1966, with James B. Beam Distilling becoming part of American Brands. Three years later Jim Beam became the best-selling bourbon in America, and a major boost in capital spending gave the company better facilities and increased warehouse space—enough to hold 850,000 barrels at a time by the end of 1975.

The Beam company managed to thrive during the lean bourbon years that extended from the late 1970s through the 1980s, even expanding its portfolio by acquiring National Distillers in 1987, along with its well-known bourbon brands, Old Grand-Dad, Old Crow, and Old Taylor.

The introduction of the Small Batch Bourbon Collection in the late 1980s was followed by the acquisition of premium brands of other types of spirits from abroad, including The Dalmore whisky from Scotland and A. de Fussigny Cognac from France.

In 1998 American Brands became Fortune Brands, and Beam achieved further globalization through a joint venture called Maxxium Worldwide in 1999—with Rémy Cointreau of France and Highland Distillers of Scotland—and the creation of Future Brands in 2001. In 2005 Beam acquired the Maker's Mark brand.

Beam bourbons include: Baker's, Basil Hayden's, Booker's, Jim Beam, Knob Creek, Old Crow, Old Grand-Dad, Old Taylor

Other Beam brands include: The Dalmore Single Highland Malt Scotch whisky, Geyser Peak wines, Lord Calvert Canadian whisky

A. SMITH BOWMAN
Fredericksburg, Virginia

The story of this distillery sounds so familiar: a farmer plants crops, harvests them, makes whiskey out of them. Only this is not a piece of land in Kentucky. And the time is not the 18th century.

A. Smith Bowman made his fortune by selling motor coaches out of Indiana. Then in 1927 he bought a 7,000-acre property in Fairfax County, Virginia, that has since been engulfed by the town of Reston. On that farm, which had an oak forest that could be used for barreling, he raised corn, rye, and barley—all valuable for whiskey making.

And that's just what he decided to do after Prohibition ended, building a distillery that opened in 1935. Virginia Gentleman bourbon became popular in our nation's capital, and during World War II Gen. Douglas MacArthur had his own supply shipped overseas.

In 1988 the distillery moved 60 miles away to the city of Fredericksburg, where its product is still the only major bourbon made outside of Kentucky—although the whiskey has its beginnings in Frankfort, where it is first distilled at Buffalo Trace. (Both Virginia Gentleman and Buffalo Trace are owned by Sazerac Company.)

After the first distillation at Buffalo Trace, the whiskey goes to Virginia, where Bowman distills it a final time and puts it in barrels for aging.

Bowman bourbons include: Virginia Gentleman

Other Bowman brands include: Bowman's rum, vodka, gin, tequila, and Canadian whisky

PARKER BEAM

Parker Beam, master distiller *for Heaven Hill, belongs to the legendary bourbon family, but he has never worked for the Jim Beam company. Neither has his son, Craig, who is also a master distiller at Heaven Hill. Neither did his father, Earl, who was also a master distiller at Heaven Hill. And neither did his grandfather Park, who was also a master distiller at Heaven Hill, as well as the brother of Jim Beam.*

With the name of Beam, you were sort of destined to be a distiller. I don't know what else you would have done. You would have been disowned. I told somebody, if you'd been a hog you'd still have become a distiller if your name was Beam.

But it's been great for the family. We pride ourselves on making the great bourbon that the Beams have been known to produce over the years.

We always like to say that every barrel at Heaven Hill whiskey has been made by Beam. That's something Beam can't say. When Booker [Noe, grandson of James Beam and a master distiller at one of the Beam facilities] came in, my dad used to say, "Who the hell's ever heard of Noe whiskey?" That's kind of a family joke there.

When we get together at family reunions, of course, we drink bourbon. Everybody drinks their own. When Baker [Parker's first cousin and a former Beam master distiller who has a bourbon, Baker's, named after him] comes over to my house, he's got a bottle of his whiskey here. I was down to his house last Sunday for a graduation party for his grandson, and he had my Evan Williams bourbon set up there on his bar. That's kind of the way we do it.

We're all partial to our own products. Nothing wrong with that. I guess if we didn't have anything of our own to drink, we'd drink each other's. As Booker said, "Hell, it's all good. Some of it's just a little better." That's what Dad used to say, too.

*The older I get, I get better at knowing
what I like and what I dislike in bourbons.*

My first memory of bourbon was that you have to acquire a sense of what you're tasting. It was, I guess, an experience that everybody would go through the first time. You think, "Man, this is much different than anything I've tasted or drunk." So it's one of those things that you acquire a taste for and a nose for, and you come to appreciate it over the years.

I think as you mature this adds more of an appreciation. That's been my experience over the years. The older I get, I think, I get better at knowing what I like and what I dislike in bourbons.

I enjoy it more, it seems like. I drink most of my bourbons all neat now. I think that's one of the changes I see in myself. Just a splash of water behind. It used to be I'd have it over the rocks. I think that as I mature I like the taste of it better.

I practically grew up in the business, from just about when I was able to walk. I went to Heaven Hill just out of high school. I have spent till 2 in the morning washing mash cookers. Dad would be out there making damn sure it was clean.

Today the master distiller doesn't hardly have to get down and get dirty. He has more of a support system when something breaks down. Back then, when a pump broke down, he was expected to help fix it. I have seen my father get greasy and dirty. The difference is that some of the early distilleries were doing 600 bushels a day versus 7,000 bushels a day now.

I'm not sure I can single out one thing that most affects the way bourbon turns out. I think it takes a combination, from grain selection to the mashbill to the distilling equipment to the fermenters, and also the aging.

The three most important things are the type of yeast you use, the type of distilling equipment you use, and the kind of warehousing you use. But you have to pay attention to all those characteristics in the process to have that good end result. You can't slight any one of them.

When you finish distilling, you don't know where that whiskey is going to wind up—in a bottle of six-year-old or ten-year-old, or in a blend. What you have to do is produce the same quality standards day in and day out. A distiller strains for consistency.

BROWN-FORMAN
Louisville, Kentucky, & Versailles, Kentucky

"A foolish consistency," Ralph Waldo Emerson said, "is the hobgoblin of little minds."

The great American philosopher would have considered the breakthrough achieved in the 1870s by whiskey seller George Garvin Brown as a wise consistency. Drinking, Emerson maintained, "insulates us in thought, whilst it unites us in feeling."

Thanks to Brown, people like Emerson could move directly from spirits to spirituality without fear of getting a whiskey that might have been either poisonous or merely disgusting in flavor. Brown did something that seems almost mundane today, because everybody in the liquor industry followed his lead.

What did Brown do? He put his whiskey in bottles.

To understand the profundity of this, you have to understand that the standard practice in those days was to put new whiskey in barrels and send it on its way. It might travel untouched, all the way to a tavern keeper or a retailer, who would then pour off a bottle or a jug's worth for a customer. Or maybe along the journey an unscrupulous person might dilute the whiskey with water or something nasty or something downright life-threatening, simply to increase profits. Anyone offended or injured by this practice would likely blame the original producer.

Brown saw the sleazy side of the whiskey business while working for a wholesale drug company in Louisville that dealt in medicinal whiskey, and he decided that the only way to ensure quality to customers was to sell in sealed bottles.

In 1870 24-year-old George Garvin Brown went into business with his half-brother, John Thompson Street Brown, as J. T. S. Brown & Brother, to specialize in the sale of bottled

All bourbon is bottled now, but the practice was introduced in 1870 by George Garvin Brown, a founder of Brown-Forman, to convince customers that the whiskey they bought had not been adulterated.

whiskey. They called their brand Old Forrester, after a local physician named William Forrester. (Later, the spelling shifted to "Forester.")

The company bought whiskeys from reputable distillers and combined them in such a way that the finished product was always the same. George Garvin Brown was his own master blender, as his son, Owsley Brown, described in the company's history, *Nothing Better in the World*, published in 1970.

"The blender would empty a certain number of barrels," Owsley Brown remembered, "then he'd bring my father some … and have him taste it." George Garvin Brown would then suggest which whiskey should be added to get the right product.

Within a few short years, J. T. S. Brown was out and George Forman was in—eventually Forman's name would be added to the name of

the company. By the time Prohibition went into effect, the business, which had begun with the blending and bottling of whiskeys made by other companies—a process called rectifying—had moved into distilling.

In a move that helped the company survive the dry period that lasted from 1919 to 1933, Owsley Brown obtained one of six permits issued nationwide that allowed whiskey to be distilled for medicinal purposes. During the dry spell Brown-Forman bought the Early Times company, thereby gaining access to its stock of whiskey so that they could meet the demand for these prescription products.

These moves allowed Brown-Forman to come out of Prohibition in a very competitive position. In 1940 the company bought the Labrot & Graham distillery near Versailles, which would later be renamed the Woodford Reserve Distillery. In 1955 they built the Early Times Distillery, which would later become the Old Forester Distillery, in the Louisville suburb of Shively.

While almost every other bourbon distiller was eventually taken over by a larger company, the Brown family continued to own and operate Brown-Forman. The company has broadened its portfolio with the acquisition of other spirits, such as Jack Daniel's, and other types of consumer goods.

Brown-Forman bourbons include: Old Forester, Woodford Reserve

Other Brown-Forman brands include: Apple-

ton Estate rum, Bolla wines, Finlandia vodkas, Jack Daniel's Tennessee whiskey

BUFFALO TRACE
Frankfort, Kentucky

Talk about a home where the buffalo roamed. Before Kentucky was settled by whites, buffalo ran wild, cutting pathways—or "traces"—through the land that would eventually be followed and broadened by human travelers. This distillery is located on the site of the Great Buffalo Trace, which was a clearing along the Kentucky River.

A settlement called Leestown formed here late in the 18th century, and a distillery was up

A number of distillers survived Prohibition because they were allowed to make and store whiskey in warehouses for medicinal purposes.

and running not long after—some sources say this happened as early as 1787. The lineage of Buffalo Trace connects to the first steam-powered distillery, built here in 1857.

Just after the end of the Civil War, Col. Benjamin Blanton first made whiskey on this site. A few years later Edmund Haynes Taylor Jr., one of the great distillers of the time and a grandnephew of President Zachary Taylor, took control of the distillery, one of three he would run at various times in this part of Kentucky. (Old Taylor, a bourbon he named after himself, is now made by Jim Beam.)

During an economic downturn in 1884, Taylor sought a loan from a friend, George T. Stagg. (Buffalo Trace sells a whiskey that bears his name.) In *The Evolution of the Bourbon Whiskey Industry in Kentucky*, Sam Cecil describes Stagg as "not-too-trustworthy," since he foreclosed on the loan to his friend, which led, understandably, to a falling-out.

Taylor witnessed and helped to further the transition to a more professional, consistent way of making whiskey. He lobbied successfully for the kind of honest labeling that was a major goal of the Bottled-in-Bond Act of 1897.

Benjamin Blanton's son Albert began working as a clerk in 1897, and he eventually became the principal owner of what was known as the

Distilleries are beautifully maintained, and not just to please those taking tours, but because any contamination can lead to bourbon that smells and tastes downright strange, if not nasty.

Albert B. Blanton Distillery. (Buffalo Trace makes a whiskey, Blanton's, in his honor.)

The distillery was mothballed when Prohibition began, but Blanton had the foresight to get a permit that allowed him to store, bottle, and distribute medicinal spirits. After Repeal, the operation was leased to Schenley Industries, with Blanton staying as manager.

After weathering problems with overproduction and the decline in bourbon consumption, the plant, which had become the Ancient Age Distillery in 1969, was sold to New York investors in 1972. The Ancient Age company was sold to a Japanese company in 1992, while the distillery itself was purchased by Sazerac, a New Orleans

ELMER T. LEE

Elmer T. Lee, the master distiller *emeritus at Buffalo Trace, developed the first single-barrel bourbon, Blanton's, in 1984. He started in the distilling business in 1949, after serving in the military during World War II, and spent his entire career at the plant in Frankfort. Lee "retired" from the distillery in 1986 but continues to work there on a regular basis.*

Come World War II, like a lot of young men, I went to service for four years. It was the old Army Air Corps. Then I took the GI Bill of Rights benefits and went to school at the University of Kentucky and studied engineering. I took what was called "power," which was the generation and distribution of electricity. That was my specialty, but it was a general mechanical-type course of study.

Come near graduation time, I started thinking about where I was going to work. The Buffalo Trace plant, which was then called the Stagg Distillery, was expanding and growing like crazy. Following World War II there was a big boom in the spirits industry—there was a lot of building, a lot of modernizing, a lot of control devices being installed—and they needed the talents of engineers.

This was in my own hometown [of Frankfort]. My father was a tobacco farmer in the area; he passed away with the typhoid fever when I was only 11 years old. My mother, after my father's death, moved into town to take employment and raise a couple of boys. So I knew a lot of people who worked [at Buffalo Trace], knew it was a good place to work, and I accepted a job and have been there ever since.

When I started I was one of the engineers who was assigned to various modernizing projects. I did that for about five years, then I was made the plant engineer. I was there for about seven years, working on new construction and the maintenance of the facilities and grounds.

All of the projects that I was assigned to were generally in the distilling or aging process, and I couldn't help but become acquainted with them. I learned a great deal about the making and the maturing and the bottling of bourbon.

After I was the plant engineer for quite a number of years, I was offered a spot being the plant superintendent. So I did that for two or three years, I guess, then I was made the plant manager.

I became more directly involved in the making of whiskey as the plant superintendent and plant manager, working closely with the people who did the job. And I was given the title of the master distiller in 1968 when I became the plant manager.

Being a master distiller is an acquired skill, and it does take time and experience. You can't study it in school, and you can't learn it over the Internet. I understudied with the quality-compliance people and the warehouse superintendents and distillery superintendents. We all tasted the product, and they clued me in to what to look for and how to judge a good bourbon. You did it with repetition, many-times-over tasting.

The high-end bourbons, the ones that people are appreciating and buying more, are very close to the old-time bourbons. The high-end bourbons are very flavorful and have a good aroma, and of course they are aged generally eight or ten years or better. Some of the bourbons I've tasted that were made before the Prohibition era were very similar to some of our good high-end bourbons now.

After Prohibition the supply was extremely low, and a lot of product, as I understand it, was put on the market at a very low age and didn't have a whole lot of bourbon character to it. There were a lot of lighter-tasting and lighter-aroma bourbons on the market compared to now.

Warehouse H was one of the favorite warehouses for Colonel Blanton. (Albert Blanton worked at—and eventually owned—the Buffalo Trace facility, known by various names over the years, from 1897 to 1953.) It's where all of our Blanton's bourbon comes from.

I like Blanton's bourbon. I think it's great. But the bourbon that I prefer—the one with my name on it, I won't say it's any better than Blanton's—to my taste at least, has a little more sweetness to it.

We introduced the first single-barrel bourbon, Blanton's, in 1984. When I retired in 1986, the people who owned the plant at the time asked if they could name a bourbon after me, and I agreed provided they let me pick the bourbon. So I've been picking the bourbon ever since. It's a single barrel. I go to Warehouses I and K, generally the middle-floor levels, and pick whiskey that's anywhere from eight to ten years old.

There are slight differences in the whiskey from barrel to barrel—even ones that sit next to each other—and the only explanation for that is the wood itself. There is a difference in the oak wood coming out of trees in various locations. The wood itself has a lot of sugars, and bourbon extracts the character of that wood taste.

Elmer T. Lee is my favorite bourbon. I would be remiss to say anything else, wouldn't I? I drink it the way most folks drink their bourbon, just over some ice with a small amount of springwater. I don't like to mix it. You can get the flavor and the taste of the bourbon if you just use good springwater and a little ice to chill it down.

liquor company. The distillery adopted the name Buffalo Trace in 2001.

Buffalo Trace bourbons include: Blanton's, Buffalo Trace, Eagle Rare, Elmer T. Lee, George T. Stagg, Hancock's President's Reserve, McAfee's Benchmark, Old Charter Proprietor's Reserve, Rock Hill Farms, W. L. Weller

Other Buffalo Trace brands include: Peychaud's Bitters, Regan's Orange Bitters No. 6

FOUR ROSES
Lawrenceburg, Kentucky

The story of the Four Roses name isn't nearly as straight as its bourbon. Over the years, the company itself has given out two different versions.

The first relates to a Tennessee family, the Roses, who had four daughters and a whiskey business. According to this account, in 1888 Paul Jones Jr. purchased the rights to the Four Roses brand name from the guy who used it to honor his offspring.

The second explanation, which came later, had to do with Jones's marriage proposal to a young woman who signaled her acceptance by wearing a corsage of four roses. Some have speculated that the second story was created to shift the family emphasis so that the Joneses could keep up with the Roses.

The history of the Four Roses distillery and its namesake spirit isn't quite that tortured, but it comes close. In his book *Bourbon, Straight*, Charles K. Cowdery tries to untangle this story—and he barely makes it out alive.

The first whiskey making at this location was by "Old" Joe Payton in 1818, shortly after he put up a tent and settled down. Between then and Prohibition, the saga involving the building of the Old Joe Distillery and the adjacent Old Prentice Distillery, as well as various financial disasters and at least one fire, is dizzying.

The two operations were sold, separately or together, at least eight times over that 101-year span, with a family named Hawkins either grabbing it or letting it go five of those times. And, Cowdery says, "After Repeal, ownership of the two neighboring plants gets more confusing."

During the dry spell between 1919 and 1933, the Four Roses company survived by taking over Frankfort Distilling in 1922 and assuming that company's permit to make whiskey for medicinal purposes. Following Repeal, Four Roses became the most popular whiskey in the country.

Modern bottling lines are an industrial marvel, with empties coming in one end and full bottles, capped and with perfectly placed labels, going out the other end to be boxed for shipping.

After World War II the company was purchased by the Canadian distilling company Seagram's, which gave the Four Roses name to the beautiful distillery facility in Lawrenceburg—a group of structures built in 1911 in the Spanish mission style and now on the National Register of Historic Places.

The Seagram's whiskey business has always been anchored on the commingling of different distillates, and the Four Roses operation seemed to adopt that practice. In 1985 Four Roses master distiller Ova Haney told an oral historian that his plant made "64 different kinds of bourbon whiskeys," which came from the mingling of "different kinds of whiskeys and [different] percentages" of those whiskeys.

Nowadays the distillery uses five different yeast strains, and each will be mixed with either of two mashbills that have different proportions of corn, rye, and barley. That means that up to ten different whiskeys may be combined—in varying proportions—to achieve a final product. (Keep in mind that this would still be considered a straight bourbon because it would be constructed only from straight bourbons.)

No other distillery creates so many types of new-make spirit, and the way those spirits age at Four Roses is also distinctive. The distillery uses single-floor warehouses, which means that the whiskeys are all subject to the same swings in temperature and humidity. (Taller warehouses can have temperature differences of 15 degrees or more from the top to the bottom.) So the spirits age at the same basic pace, eliminating the need to rotate barrels within warehouses to achieve consistency.

In those warehouses where barrels range high and wide, placement can make a big difference, as warmer temperatures above will cause those whiskeys to mature at a faster pace than those below.

In the late 1950s Four Roses whiskey was taken out of the American market, even though it was still popular here, and diverted to overseas sales. That continued until the Kirin Brewery Company of Japan, where Four Roses had been a popular brand, purchased the company from Seagram's in 2002.

In September 2003, after an absence of nearly 45 years, Four Roses whiskeys were reintroduced in the United States, with distribution limited at first to Kentucky and then slowly expanded elsewhere in the country.

Four Roses bourbon brand: Four Roses
Other brands: None

HEAVEN HILL
Louisville, Kentucky

The Heaven Hill company calls Bardstown home. That's where the company started up in 1934. Today that's where the company's bottling plant and most of the warehouses are located. But since November 7, 1996, Heaven Hill has had to make its whiskey away from Bardstown.

On that night a tremendous fire—described as the worst distillery blaze Kentucky has ever seen—wiped out seven warehouses, a number of small buildings, and the stillhouse. Before the fire was brought under control, one worried customer reportedly called the local fire department and said, "Heaven Hill bottles the whiskey I drink, and I wanted to know if it was all burning up."

Faced with a severe need to keep the spirits coming, Heaven Hill turned to other distilleries for support. "They were more than glad to jump in and help us with our production needs," says Parker Beam, master distiller for Heaven Hill.

Heaven Hill moved as much materials and personnel as it could to the Early Times Distillery (now called the Old Forester Distillery) in Louisville and to the Beam operation in nearby Boston.

The all-important Heaven Hill yeast was not lost because it was in a sealed walk-in cooler that wasn't damaged in the fire, so some of the yeast was sent to Louisville to make Heaven Hill spirits in a plant normally used for Brown-Forman's needs.

At the Beam distillery in Boston, however, Heaven Hill used the yeast already found on the premises. "We felt like there were so many similarities to our yeast," says Beam. "It's the same strain that has been passed around the Beam family. We didn't feel like we had to address the issue with them."

In 1999 Heaven Hill bought the Bernheim Distillery in Louisville, a modern facility built only seven years earlier. Now the company's whiskeys are distilled about 30 miles from where they eventually are bottled.

Surviving the fire was tough, but Heaven Hill has had to overcome challenges from the very beginning. The country was still struggling with the Great Depression and the whiskey industry was coping with the aftermath of Prohibition when the Old Heavenhill Springs Distillery was started by a group of Bardstown-area investors and five Shapira brothers: David, Ed, Gary, George, and Mose.

The distillery was named after William Heavenhill, a farmer born during a 1783 Indian raid that took place on the company's property. Other than the fact that Heavenhill worked the land that would become the distillery's property, there was no connection. Apparently, a typographical error on an application form resulted in the company name Heaven Hill.

The men who founded the distillery, which started bottling in 1935, were in the dry-goods business and had no working knowledge of bourbon making, but they had the assistance of Joe Beam, a cousin to Jim Beam. Joe Beam's son, Harry, was master distiller from early on, followed by one of Harry's cousins, Earl, in 1946. In 1975 Earl's son, Parker, became master distiller, and his son, Craig Beam, began to share the responsibilities with him in recent years.

Joined by the Homel family in 1942, the Shapira family continues to own and operate Heaven Hill.

Labrot & Graham's limestone rackhouses, dating from 1812, Versailles, Kentucky

Heaven Hill bourbons include: Cabin Still, Echo Spring, Elijah Craig, Evan Williams, Fighting Cock, Heaven Hill, Henry McKenna, Kentucky Deluxe, J. W. Dant, Mattingly & Moore, Old Fitzgerald, T. W. Samuels

Other Heaven Hill brands include: Christian Brothers brandy, Hpnotiq liqueur, Isle of Jura Scotch whisky, Kilbeggan Irish whiskey, Tyrconnell Irish whiskey

MAKER'S MARK
Loretto, Kentucky

The makers of bourbon love their traditions. Maybe that's because virtually all of them are from Kentucky, where the distilling of bourbon is so deeply embedded in the history of the commonwealth, and maybe that's because the making of bourbon has been such a family affair, with the craft of distilling being passed down along the generations.

But in 1953 Bill Samuels Sr. torched such sentimental notions—literally—by taking the family recipe that had been around for 170 years and burning it in a conference room at the distillery in Loretto.

"Nothing that we need!" he proclaimed. "To craft a truly new and soft-spoken bourbon, we will have to start from scratch."

This revolutionary act had an unintended consequence. According to Bill Samuels Jr. in his book *Maker's Mark: My Autobiography*, Bill Samuels Sr. accidentally set the drapes on fire.

That was the rebirth of the Samuels distilling operation. The birth had occurred in 1780 when Robert Samuels—the great-great-great-great-grandfather of Bill Jr.—moved from Pennsylvania to Kentucky to farm and distill. His grandson Taylor Williams Samuels started the family's first commercial distillery, T. W. Samuels and Son, on the family farm at Deatsville in 1844.

T. W. Samuels enjoyed great success, achieving national distribution for his whiskeys. His grandson Leslie Samuels was in charge of the company when the distillery and six warehouses burned down in 1909. With money from a Cincinnati investor, the distillery was rebuilt, only to be torn down after the onset of Prohibition.

In 1933 Leslie Samuels reorganized the company and rebuilt the facility as the T. W. Samuels Distillery with another Cincinnati investor, who decided to sell it in 1943. This caused his son, Bill Samuels Sr. (another T. W. Samuels), to leave the whiskey business until 1953, when he bought the old Burks Spring Distillery and went for the burn.

*Bourbon has to be matured in new oak barrels to satisfy legal requirements,
and the interaction between the maturing whiskey and the wood gets off to a strong start.*

While the destruction of the old recipe was ceremonial, the introduction of the new recipe brought a major change: the elimination of rye as a flavor grain and its replacement with wheat. The reformulated bourbon that was introduced in 1958 as Maker's Mark was softer and less spicy than the whiskey previously made by the Samuels family.

Sales of Maker's Mark were slow in the first years after its introduction, but it has gradually become a strong force in the marketplace. In 1981 the distillery was sold to Hiram Walker, a company taken over in 1987 by Allied-Lyons, which became Allied-Domecq after a 1994 merger. The 2005 breakup of Allied-Domecq put Maker's Mark into the hands of the Beam company.

Through all of these changes, Bill Samuels Jr. has remained a steadying force as the president of the company. Even as the company has grown bigger, he continues to think small, as in the production of one single whiskey in small batches.

Maker's Mark bourbon brand: Maker's Mark
Other brands: None

PRICHARD'S DISTILLERY
Kelso, Tennessee

Phil Prichard was a dental technician for 30 years, and then he needed to do something else. That dissatisfaction lead Prichard and his wife, Connie, to start Prichard's Distillery, and it has been making rum in pot stills, using premium-grade sorghum molasses, since 1997. It would seem natural for Prichard's to make Tennessee whiskey, but with Jack Daniel's about 15 miles away, and George Dickel another 30 or so past that, Prichard decided to go a different way: bourbon, distilled in Kentucky and aged for a while there, then shipped to Tennessee for some more time in wood. Prichard has plans to make his own whiskey, but with the new product he will, again, take a different direction—it will be a single-malt whiskey made from barley.

WILD TURKEY
Lawrenceburg, Kentucky

The saga of Wild Turkey is like one of those old-time movie romances in which opposites attract. In this case the couple was the result of blending Kentucky distilling savvy with East Coast marketing skill. But it took a while for the two to meet.

Our story begins in Kentucky. Sometime in the 1830s two brothers, John and James Ripy, arrive near Lawrenceburg, in a place they name Tyrone after the county in Ireland where they were born. By 1851 they open a store that sells general goods. The settlement of Tyrone would eventually fade from memory, but not the Ripys.

Then the scene shifts to New York. In 1855 Friend P. Fitts takes the big money he made from the California Gold Rush and bets it on a food

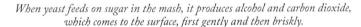

When yeast feeds on sugar in the mash, it produces alcohol and carbon dioxide, which comes to the surface, first gently and then briskly.

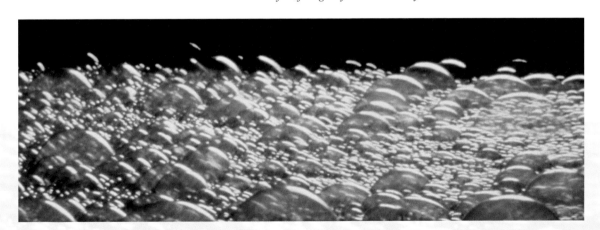

JIMMY RUSSELL

Jimmy Russell celebrated *his 50th year in bourbon in 2004, with all five of his decades spent at the same place: Wild Turkey, where he has run the distillery since the early 1960s. A special whiskey, Wild Turkey Tribute, was issued in a very limited quantity to mark the occasion. In recent years, Russell has been grooming his son Eddie to become the master distiller at the Wild Turkey Distillery.*

I live here in what's called Bourbon Country. I was born and raised in Lawrenceburg. There were four or five distilleries here when I was growing up. You just grow up around the whiskey, because many people you knew worked at the distilleries.

I probably tried bourbon for the first time when I was about 16, 17, 18—somewhere about there. I can't really say what I thought of the taste. It was something like when a bunch of boys are running around together. If they can get a bottle, they all have a drink out of it. I must have liked it pretty well. But we did not consume it like that in the home, no sir.

My father worked at a distillery. He was a maintenance supervisor, and he took care of the equipment and things like that. He started out with the Old Joe Distilling Company, and he finished up till he retired at the Wild Turkey Distillery.

There were some 40-odd distilleries when I started out in 1954 in Kentucky, and we're down to eight or nine now. Over the years, the smaller ones were bought up by the bigger ones, and there's been [distillery] consolidations and label consolidations and things. There's still a lot of the brands out there, but they're made by different distilleries. I doubt that these whiskeys have any relation to what they used to be like.

My grandfather also worked in a distillery—before Prohibition but not after Prohibition. Really, I don't know what he did. That was a long time ago, in the early 1900s. It was called the Saffel Distillery [located north of Lawrenceburg, until it went out of business when Prohibition went into effect].

In the early 1950s it was a lot of family-owned distilleries, but the costs became too much. It's like grocery stores—when I was growing up there were a lot of family-owned grocery stores in Lawrenceburg. Now we've got Kroger. Family-owned businesses can't compete with bigger corporations.

When I started out at the distillery, they told me I'd be working in quality control. Back in that day quality control meant that you might be checking that load of grain that came in. And then you might end

up with a scoop shovel, helping to unload that truck. You had a job, but also you did a little bit of everything else that needed to be done. I spent several years actually running equipment in the distillery and the bottling operations and everything. I've had a general view of the whole operation.

Usually in the bourbon business, wherever you start is where you stay. Say if you start in the distillation end of it, that's basically where you stay all the time, or in the aging process, or in the bottling process. That's the way it was. You don't move.

But that wasn't what happened with me. I didn't really know what was going on. I suppose they must have liked something I was doing, so I spent time getting to know all the jobs.

You know, when you get used to doing something, you get to a point you relax a little bit. You know what to do all the time. And when I would get to that point, and think I had it made, well, they would move me to another department. Then I had to learn that all over again. But I've been fortunate to have experience in the distillation, the aging, the bottling, and everything.

I became the master distiller in the late 1960s. The old gentleman who was the master distiller here before me, he more or less took me under his wing and started training me. Then, when he retired, they moved me up to the master distiller's job.

[The apprenticeship] was enjoyable. In a small community, you're working with people you've known all your life. The older people there, they had known me since I was a little boy. It was like working with a family. You knew everybody. You were friends with the young people; you went to school with them.

Now my son's here with me. He's been here 25 years. And I've done him the same way they did me—train him in all phases of the operation. You know what each step's going to be, and what the next step is, and what the final step is. I've been fortunate that that's the way I was trained. And he's been trained the same way.

I think that being good at what I do is a combination of a natural ability and learning through experience. You know, a lot of people can taste something—food, bourbons, anything—and say this doesn't taste right. You've got to know in the tasting what's wrong. Is it not stored high enough in the storage building to be aging like you want it to be? Or is it stored too high and does it need to be moved down? All of us can tell whether it tastes good or tastes bad, but you have to know why it tastes like that.

company in New York that would eventually be known as Austin, Nichols & Co.

Back to Kentucky, almost 20 years later. A son of James Ripy is about to commence a brilliant career in whiskey. Thomas B. Ripy—known as T. B.—would become a major figure in Anderson County. In 1869 he buys a year-old distillery with a single partner who would soon move on.

T. B. Ripy's success spurs a series of moves. According to Gary Regan and Mardee Haidin Regan's *The Book of Bourbon*, "By 1880 the company had reportedly moved to larger accommodations a full five times." In 1893 a Ripy whiskey is chosen over 400 other entries to represent Kentucky at the 1893 World's Columbian Exposition in Chicago.

Ripy continues to buy and sell distilleries with a flair, and by the time he dies in 1905 his sons have taken over another distillery in Lawrenceburg. The *Anderson County News* says that "The whiskey made at the Ripy Distillery has been tested and endorsed in almost every village and hamlet of the land." It goes on to boast about the younger generation, saying that they have "had much experience under their able father."

Not enough, however, to survive Prohibition. The plant is almost entirely torn down, to be rebuilt in 1937 as the Ripy Bros. Distillery. Although the facility changes hands several times, over the years a Ripy always seems to be working there.

Meanwhile, back in New York, after Repeal the head of Austin, Nichols & Co. decides to expand into the alcohol business, and he pays distilleries to make a line of spirits for him. In the early 1940s this man, Thomas McCarthy, takes a bottle of his bourbon on a trip to hunt wild turkey in South Carolina. After his friends keep requesting more of that "wild turkey bourbon," the brand name is born.

Finally, a match is made in bourbon heaven. Austin, Nichols & Co. buys the old Ripy distillery in 1972 and renames it the Boulevard Distillery. At this time the distillery manager is Jimmy Russell, who learned his trade in the early 1950s from Ernest W. Ripy Jr. Not only would Russell become a legendary master distiller, but he would stay put. In 2004 he celebrated his 50th year on the job in Lawrenceburg.

Austin, Nichols & Co. was taken over in 1980 by Groupe Pernod Ricard, a French company that is now one of the biggest liquor concerns in the world. Its brands include Chivas Regal Scotch whisky, Jameson Irish whiskey, Martell cognac, Ricard pastis, and The Glenlivet Scotch whisky. At the end of 2001 the Lawrenceburg facility was renamed the Wild Turkey Distillery.

Wild Turkey bourbon brand: Wild Turkey
Other brands: None

Down a rackhouse aisle of aging barrels, Buffalo Trace Distillery, Franklin County, Kentucky

OTHER PRODUCERS

Some of these companies have a deep and enduring connection to the bourbon business. Others just began to sell whiskey as the market for more expensive products, such as these, started to show strong growth.

In the old days a rectifier was somebody who processed whiskey, or whiskeys, from one or more distilleries. Often these companies diluted straight bourbons to produce blended American whiskeys by combining straights with blander spirits.

The companies included here sell straight bourbon whiskey. Some of these producers may combine whiskeys from different distilleries, or they may mingle different whiskeys from the same distillery, but if all the components of the final product are straight bourbon whiskeys, then the final product can be called a straight bourbon whiskey.

In Scotland, independent (or third-party) bottlers do something comparable with single malts, although in most cases the name of the original whisky distillery will be mentioned on the label along with the name of the bottler.

That's not the practice here in the States. Our labels include only the name of the producer.

Unless the whiskey is being released as a single-barrel bourbon, various barrels are dumped and then subjected to the blender's art.

A rectifier was somebody who processed whiskey, or whiskeys, from one or more distilleries.

CHATHAM IMPORTS
New York, New York

CLASSIC CASK
Sunrise, Florida

Although the company was set up about 30 years ago, Joseph J. Magliocco has been operating it as a broad-based spirits, wine, and beer business for just around 15 years. Chatham's brands include a flavored rum brand, Martí Auténtico, as well as a number of high-end Bordeaux, Italian, Spanish, Australian, and Argentinian wines, and New Amsterdam beer.

Chatham started selling whiskeys under the Michter's label in 2000. At first the company used spirits that had already been produced, but in 2001 it began to commission the distillation of spirits itself. When these whiskeys reach maturity, they will be sold as Michter's. "We wanted to produce whiskeys that would have a certain 'house' style," says Magliocco, "the sort of whiskey that we like to drink ourselves."

Classic Cask was introduced in 1999 by Alan Shayne, who has several different lines of high-end spirits. In addition to bourbon, the Classic Cask collection includes rye whiskeys and single-cask, single-malt Scotch whiskies.

Rather than promoting brands that have one consistent style, Shayne brings out limited editions of special bottlings. In the case of bourbon, his blender in Bardstown, Kentucky, has created a series of small batches that are available only as long as supplies last. In 2004 Classic Cask introduced a 13-year-old bourbon, and when it has sold out, another whiskey will come on the market.

Shayne's better-known venture is the Scotch Malt Whisky Society of America, which is a for-profit company organized as a club. Members can buy special cask-strength bottlings of Scotch single-malt whiskies that aren't available anywhere else. "We try to stay top of the line with everything we do," says Shayne, president of the society, which is the North American branch of the Scotland-based Scotch Malt Whisky Society.

Fermentation was traditionally carried out in tanks made of cypress, which was a neutral material, but except for a handful of distilleries, such as Wild Turkey, shown here, stainless steel is now the standard.

CORNER CREEK DISTILLING
Miami, Florida

Since he first started working in the liquor business in the 1970s, Ted Kraut has watched a lot of strange things happen. And maybe that helps to explain why, in the late 1990s, he saw how badly the bourbon market was doing—and decided to give it a try anyway.

"I was sitting with my future partner, Eliot Levin, and we were talking about how the bottom had fallen out," Kraut remembers. "I said, 'Now is the time to get into premium bourbon.'"

Kraut and Levin found their whiskey at a blending company in Bardstown, and they introduced Corner Creek Reserve Bourbon Whiskey in 1999. It is a major label for the partnership, which imports King Lager from Australia, but a small operation compared to the liquor business in general.

In fact, Corner Creek will bottle to order, if that will make its distributors and retailers happy. "If you call up and say, 'I need 70 cases,'" Kraut says, "I will make it for you."

CVI BRANDS
San Carlos, California

CVI has been in the liquor business since the end of the 1970s, but it didn't begin to sell its own line of bourbons—and one rye—under the Black Maple Hill brand until the turn of the 21st century. Armagnacs and single-malt Scotch whiskies dominate the CVI portfolio.

"We like to find bourbons of a fuller, richer style with a long finish," CVI president Paul Joseph says. "With bourbon, as with all of our products, we search for extraordinary quality."

DAVID SHERMAN CORPORATION
St. Louis, Missouri

The David Sherman Corporation began in 1958 as a private-label bottler of distilled spirits, but it has since broadened its business to include the import and export of liquor and wine brands. Their portfolio includes Everclear neutral spirits, Margaritaville tequila, Pearl vodka, and Arrow cordials.

DIAGEO
London, England

Diageo is the largest alcohol seller in the world. It owns and/or distributes 9 of the top 20 global liquor brands, including Smirnoff vodka, Guinness stout, Tanqueray gin, and Johnnie Walker Scotch whisky. In Scotland alone the company owns more than 30 whisky distilleries.

So you'd think that Diageo, which was created when two giant companies merged in 1997, would have a distillery where it makes bourbon. But it doesn't. Diageo obtained its bourbon brand, Bulleit, in 1999 as part of the breakup of the Seagram's liquor empire. Bulleit had been made at the Buffalo Trace Distillery for Seagram's, but it is now made for Diageo at the Four Roses Distillery.

DRINKS AMERICAS
Wilton, Connecticut

The senior management of Drinks Americas includes two former Seagram's executives who helped to form the company in 2002, the same year it purchased the Old Whiskey River bourbon brand. The company also has Cohete rum, Aguila tequila, Normans wines, and Y Saké among its liquor brands, as well as Newman's Own Lightly Sparkling Fruit Juices and Swiss T among its nonalcoholic products.

KENTUCKY BOURBON DISTILLERS
Bardstown, Kentucky

This company traces its beginnings to a time shortly after the Civil War and a man named John David Willett. He formed a partnership in

Bardstown with a group of men that included Thomas S. Moore (later of Mattingly & Moore fame). That partnership ended when Willett fell ill and had to sell his share.

The next generation, however, kept on distilling. Working with his father, Willett's son Lambert had started in the whiskey business when he was 15. He went on to the Moore & Selliger Distillery—with George Moore—in Louisville before Prohibition, raised hogs and cattle on his farm in Bardstown during the dry spell, and returned to Moore & Selliger (now operated by Heaven Hill) once drinking became legal again.

Lambert Willett's son Thompson worked with him at Moore & Selliger before leaving to start the Willett Distilling Company in 1935 on

Charring the insides of a barrel creates a red layer that gives bourbon some of its flavor and all of its rich color while the whiskey matures.

the outskirts of Bardstown. Thompson's brother John, an engineer, designed the facility. Four more brothers—Paul, Bill, Charles, and Robert—would eventually work for the company.

In the late 1970s the operation split, with the Willetts continuing to warehouse whiskey while the distillery was converted to a fuel-alcohol plant. Although the energy crisis of the 1970s made the plant seem like a promising opportunity, the business went bankrupt by the end of the decade.

In 1984 a son-in-law of Thompson Willett named Even Kulsveen reestablished the family's bourbon operation. He has built a very successful bottling operation creating whiskeys for many of the independent bottlers, and he sells his own products as Kentucky Bourbon Distillers.

In the early years of the 21st century, Kulsveen began renovations at the old Willett facility with the intention of resuming distillation.

McLAIN & KYNE
Louisville, Kentucky

There is no McLain. There is no Kyne. There is no distillery. But there is a hardworking young man named Trey Zoeller who entered the whiskey business in the mid-1990s after several years working in sales for a long-distance telephone company and a number of health care–related firms.

Zoeller grew up in Louisville, Kentucky, but went away for college and various jobs. After returning home, he bought a supply of bourbon from one distillery that shall remain nameless and then had it bottled at another anonymous distillery.

The whiskeys he introduced in 1998 were called Jefferson's Reserve and Sam Houston. Two more bourbons—Jefferson's and Very Old Jefferson's Reserve—followed in 2003.

Later that same year Zoeller started another company, Phoenix Global Group, that sells energy drinks, including one called Vegas and one called Pink. In 2007 the company was sold to Castle Brands, but Zoeller continues to run it.

Although there isn't a McLain or a Kyne at the company, the names belong to two of Zoeller's ancestors who made moonshine whiskey long, long ago. In fact, his great-great-great-grandmother McLain was arrested for illegal distilling. "Those are the roots of this business—moonshine," Zoeller says. "They just didn't want to pay taxes."

That's one part of the family tradition Zoeller does not carry on.

THE OLD POGUE DISTILLERY
Bardstown, Kentucky

H. E. Pogue was the master distiller of the Old Time Distillery in Maysville, Kentucky, in the late 1860s, and he took over the company in 1876. One of the brands H. E. Pogue produced was Old Pogue Kentucky Straight Bourbon Whiskey.

Pogue's whiskeys developed a following out West. Orders came in from as far away as Arizona, and famed Western artist Charles M. Russell depicted a case of a Pogue whiskey in his 1909 painting *In without Knocking*.

The family business experienced tragedy as well as triumph. H. E. Pogue and his son, H. E. Pogue II, died in separate distillery accidents—the father in 1890 and the son in 1918. H. E. Pogue III was serving in the Navy when he received notice that his father had been killed, and he came home to take over the operation.

Although the company was able to sell some whiskey for medicinal purposes during the early years of Prohibition, it went into decline and was sold in 1935.

In 1996, six descendants of H. E. Pogue I, including H. E. Pogue IV and H. E. Pogue V, came together to revive the brand, which led to the introduction of Old Pogue Master's Select in 2004.

"We wanted to put this together as a fun project to get us together more often than at Christmas and Thanksgiving," says Jack Pogue, who is a Firestone tires dealer in Campbellsville, Kentucky. "It turned into something more."

OLD RIP VAN WINKLE DISTILLERY
Frankfort, Kentucky

In *Bluegrass, Belles, and Bourbon*, Harry Harrison Kroll calls Julian Van Winkle "the last of the great old distillers." Van Winkle, who was known to all as Pappy, began as a salesman for the W. L. Weller & Sons whiskey operation in 1893.

By 1908 he and a partner took control of the company and then absorbed the John A. Fitzgerald Distillery. Weller survived Prohibition as one of the few distilleries allowed to make medicinal whiskeys, and just before Repeal the company took over the A. Ph. Stitzel Distillery, becoming the Stitzel-Weller Distillery. Its major brands at the time were W. L. Weller, Old Fitzgerald, Cabin Still, and Rebel Yell.

Pappy Van Winkle continued running the company almost until his death in 1965 at the age of 91. His son, Julian Van Winkle Jr., took over, but in 1972 stockholders voted to sell the distillery and the rights to all of the company's brands.

Soon after that, using stocks of whiskeys that had been produced at the Stitzel-Weller Distillery, Van Winkle resurrected a brand, Old Rip Van Winkle, that his family still owned. When he passed away in 1981, his son Julian Van Winkle III began to run the company, and he does so today with the help of his son Preston Van Winkle.

In 2002 Julian III started a joint venture with Buffalo Trace, which now makes all of the whiskeys for the Old Rip Van Winkle brands.

PREISS IMPORTS
Ramona, California

Among the dozens of brands that he brings into the United States, Henry Preiss has several spirits that are considered legendary. These include single malts made by the Spring-bank distillery in Campbelltown, Scotland; the maraschino liqueur made by Luxardo in Torreg-

lia, Italy; and the Armagnacs of François Darroze, distilled in what was once the Gascony province in southwestern France.

But Preiss has only one bourbon—and it is a singular one at that. While Pennsylvania was a major center of whiskey making in the early years of the United States, all of its distilleries are now gone. The last one was Michter's, located in Schaefferstown, but it went out of business in 1988. All of the whiskey from Michter's that is still available commercially is bottled by Preiss Imports under the brand name of A. H. Hirsch.

"There isn't much of it left," Henry Preiss says, "and once it's gone, it's gone."

The great-great-great-grandmother of Trey Zoeller, founder of McLain & Kyne, was arrested for illegal distilling. "Those are the roots of this business—moonshine," Zoeller says.

Relic still located on the Labrot & Graham property, Versailles, Kentucky

CHAPTER FOUR

A GUIDE TO THE BOURBONS
The Yearning Palate

So what does this stuff taste like? And is it worth the money?
Well, by and large, the answers are: very nice and yes.

It's hard to generalize, because the range of flavors and aromas is quite astonishing. Caramel and vanilla are almost universal, but many bourbons have accents of fruit (cherry, apricot, apple), spice (black pepper, cinnamon, mint), and nuts (almond, walnut, hazelnut), as well as various kinds of sweetness (honey, brown sugar, corn syrup). Some flavors and aromas, such as oak, seem obvious, while others, like leather, are surprising.

Sometimes the flavors and aromas snap at you like a string of firecrackers. Others take their time, gliding from one impression to the next like a slow-motion scene in a movie. Or they may be so tightly wound that you cannot pick them apart, though you'll have great fun trying.

Drinking one of these fine spirits should take you beyond the usual experience of less-expensive bourbon in one or two ways. The flavors should be more vivid—deeper, richer, focused. And they should work together in some meaningful way, balancing one tantalizing element against another.

Those rules apply unless, of course, the whiskey is meant to be a take-no-prisoners, good ole bourbon of a higher, if not tamer, order. But even then the flavors should add up to something greater, like the cannons that come charging into the finale of the "1812 Overture."

To be fair, a number of people who produce the better bourbons listed here do not take kindly to this kind of dissection. They are not critics. They are not aesthetes. They make bourbon that they like, maybe even love, but always enjoy. Their whiskeys may be erudite, but these folks speak plainly.

Asked to describe the taste of the stuff sold by Kentucky Bourbon Distillers—produced, essentially, by his father, Even—Drew Kulsveen says, "We don't believe in that BS. We make *bourbon*." (He might not have emphasized it enough to deserve the italics, but that's what he *meant*.)

Now, about the cost. Everything is relative. You can buy some pleasant bourbon for very little money: under $10 for a 750-milliliter bottle. You can find some of the treasures listed here for under $20. Many more for under $30. Some, certainly, for more than $50. Very few for more than $100. That price buys you the *most coveted bourbon in the world*. And some of it is quite rare.

Longer aging does not always mean better bourbon. To be called "straight," the whiskey must age for at least two years. If it has aged between two and four years, the label must indicate this length of time. Older spirits need not reveal their age, but almost certainly will if the whiskey has had the benefit of long exposure to wood.

The list that follows is meant to be inclusive. I have not been a size-ist. Some small batches of bourbon are smaller than others, but you cannot taste smallness. My goal is to help you learn more and make better choices when it comes to buying these whiskeys. When a whiskey was in doubt, I chose to add it to this A-to-W compendium, rather than excluding it from the list.

In some cases this task became difficult to manage. Some whiskeys come on the market in very limited quantities and sell out quickly. I have included some products that could sell out in the time it takes for this information to go from my word processor to the printed page. But, again, I have tried to err on the side of more bourbons rather than fewer.

In a few cases I give one example of a whiskey from a brand that is ever changing. Single-barrel bourbons differ from bottling to bottling because no two barrels are the same—even though the differences might be somewhat slight.

And although they may strive for consistency, some brands have a built-in changeability: with each batch, small producers who do not distill their own bourbon will choose from those whiskeys available to them. In other words, a few of these examples represent a bourbon from one particular bottling, a snapshot of one amber-colored moment in time.

With very few exceptions, the descriptions of color, aroma, and flavor come directly from the producers themselves. This was my attempt to be less of a critic and more of a gatherer and dispenser of information. Many people have brought eloquence and evocative power to their bourbon analyses—Gary Regan, Jim Murray, F. Paul Pacult, and Charles Cowdery, among them. I commend these writers to you.

But now, here, I give you the distillers on their distillations. Cheers to them and cheers to you.

A. H. HIRSCH
DISTILLER: Michter's

Call this a tale of two Michter's— a story that at times sounds like the old Abbott and Costello routine "Who's on first?" First, in this case, was a distillery in Pennsylvania named Michter's that was the last great bourbon maker in that state. After Michter's—the distillery—shut in the late 1980s, a man named Adolf Hirsch bought the remaining stock of Michter's whiskey but not the rights to the brand. The A. H. Hirsch whiskey—made by the distillery but not named for it—has changed hands at least twice. Preiss Imports now owns the dwindling supply. (For the other side of the story, see the whiskey listed under "Michter's.") Because of its scarcity, its connection

to a state that had a strong tradition of distilling, and its considerable quality, this has become a highly treasured whiskey.

Age 16 years
Proof 91.6
Color amber
Aroma toffee, vanilla, dried fruit, spice
Flavor vanilla, toffee, mint, evergreen, dried apricots

ANCIENT ANCIENT AGE
DISTILLER: Buffalo Trace

Distillery names may change, but brand names endure. The Stagg Distillery first introduced the Ancient Age brand shortly after Prohibition as a bourbon-style whiskey that was actually produced in Canada. Reconfigured after World War II as a straight bourbon, it emerged as the flagship brand of what would become the Buffalo Trace Distillery in 2001. But for more than 30 years, Ancient Age was made at the Ancient Age Distillery. There are a number of Ancient Age whiskeys, but Ancient Ancient Age refers to the longer-aged stuff.

BASIC BOURBON

T_he entry fee for bourbon is invitingly low._ Nothing else in the spirit world lets you dabble for so little money. (And, in truth, some of the better stuff is quite affordable as well.) For a lighter introduction to bourbon, those whiskeys made of wheat, as well as corn, can be soft and easy. Old Fitzgerald (86 proof), made by Heaven Hill, has mild aromas and delicate flavors of honey, grain, and citrus.

Rebel Yell (80 proof), a wheated bourbon sold by David Sherman, pushes the sensory experience without being all that aggressive. The aromas of honey, fruit, and light spice lead to flavors ranging from caramel to soft leather. The taste may be slightly more vivid, but this bourbon is still a good place to start.

Thanks to the use of rye as a secondary grain, Jim Beam's eight-year-old whiskey, bottled with a black label and known as Jim Beam Black (86 proof), takes us into territory that has a little more oomph. Honey, green pepper, and spice are among the aromas; brown sugar, oak, and orange zest are among the flavors.

Managing to be both more flavorful and more elegant, Buffalo Trace's flagship product, Buffalo Trace (90 proof), has the richness of deep vanilla and brown sugar, with a nice creamy consistency.

Heaven Hill sells a whiskey with a bit more edge, called Old Heaven Hill, at 100 proof. It shows the presence of extra rye through its spiciness, which combines nicely with caramel notes.

Old Forester 100 proof, from Brown-Forman, gives off soft aromas, but the whiskey comes right after you when you sip it. It is sweet, fruity, spicy, oaky—all arriving bam-bam-bam-bam.

Another 100-proof bourbon, Old Grand-Dad, made by Beam, also bursts with assertive aromas and flavors. Candied spice, honey, leather, corn, and caramel swoop in at first, and then they take a mellow turn.

Wild Turkey 101 proof, from the Wild Turkey Distillery, seduces you with rounded aromas of caramel, vanilla, apricot, and cinnamon. When sipped, however, the whiskey takes a bolder stand, thanks to big, vivid flavors of brown sugar, caramel, vanilla, fruit, and spice.

Age 10 years

Proof 86

Color orange-amber

Aroma deep caramel, soft vanilla, cocoa, toasted almond

Flavor deep caramel, soft vanilla, cocoa, toasted almond, leather

BAKER'S
DISTILLER: Jim Beam

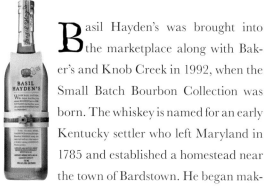

When the Beam company created the Small Batch Bourbon Collection in 1992, Baker's was one of three new whiskeys that were introduced. It is named for Baker Beam, a former master distiller at the company and son of Carl Beam, another master distiller at the company. He's also a grandnephew of Jim Beam himself. Baker Beam developed the recipe for this whiskey while working for the Beam company, from which he has retired, although he will occasionally drive a truck for the Heaven Hill distillery, where a cousin, Parker Beam, and Parker's son, Craig, work as master distillers. A note from Baker Beam on the label of his whiskey says, "My Bourbon follows our Beam family tradition of putting our best

secrets inside the bottle, not here on the label. I've distilled six generations of Bourbon skill into this bottle. That's a lot of good secrets."

Age 7 years

Proof 107

Color warm amber, tawny, nut brown

Aroma fruit, vanilla, caramel

Flavor toasted nuts, fruit, vanilla

BASIL HAYDEN'S
DISTILLER: Jim Beam

Basil Hayden's was brought into the marketplace along with Baker's and Knob Creek in 1992, when the Small Batch Bourbon Collection was born. The whiskey is named for an early Kentucky settler who left Maryland in 1785 and established a homestead near the town of Bardstown. He began making whiskey before the turn of the 18th century, and the Beam company says the recipe for this bourbon dates to that time. Hayden's grandson created the brand name Old Grand-Dad in 1882 and put Basil's image on the Old Grand-Dad label, where he still resides. Beam makes Basil Hayden's, like Old Grand-Dad, with a high percentage of rye in its mix of grains—much more than most bourbons. Though Basil Hayden's spends a little more time in barrels than Old Grand-Dad, some people see a distinct family resemblance between the two whiskeys named for the same man.

Age 8 years
Proof 80
Color golden amber
Aroma spice, tea, hint of peppermint
Flavor spice, pepper, honey

BENJAMIN PRICHARD'S DOUBLE BARRELED

DISTILLER: *Not available*

A Tennessee bourbon? Well, in a limited sense, that's what we have here. This whiskey was distilled in Kentucky and aged there for upwards of eight years before being sold to Prichard's Distillery in Kelso, Tennessee, where it was put into a new, charred, white-oak barrel for almost three more years. The idea, says the company's Phil Prichard, was to intensify the effects of the wood on the spirit.

Age 9 years
Proof 90
Color dark mahogany
Aroma toffee and wood smoke
Flavor intense, complex sweetness, with vanilla and wood smoke

BLACK MAPLE HILL

DISTILLER: *Not available*

These bourbons are bottled in Kentucky for CVI Brands of San Carlos, California. The size of the batches runs from 10 to 20 barrels.

Age 11 years
Proof 95
Color orange gold
Aroma soft vanilla, apple, caramel
Flavor vanilla, apple, caramel, oak, hazelnut—brawny

Age 14 years
Proof 95
Color red-orange-gold
Aroma vanilla, butterscotch, oak
Flavor vanilla, butterscotch, oak, cherry, spice, maple—brawny

Age 16 years
Proof 95
Color orange-gold
Aroma vanilla, cherry, toffee, black tea
Flavor vanilla, cherry, toffee, black tea—elegant

Age 21 years
Proof 95
Color red-orange-gold
Aroma vanilla, leather, cherry
Flavor vanilla, cherry, leather—earthy assertive

BLANTON'S
DISTILLER: Buffalo Trace

The better-bourbon boom began here. In the old days no one ever applied the adjective *boutique* to Kentucky straight whiskey of the predominantly corn variety. That only came years after Elmer T. Lee, the master distiller of what became Buffalo Trace in 2001, honored former master distiller Col. Albert B. Blanton, with whom Lee had worked in the 1950s. The colonel started working at the distillery as an office boy in 1897, then became its manager in 1912. In 1953, when Blanton retired, the distillery was renamed in his honor. Barrels that become Blanton's are generally six to eight years old.

Age no age statement (single barrel)
Proof 93
Color amber
Aroma caramel, dried fruit, vanilla, marshmallow
Flavor caramel, vanilla, dried fruit, spice, tobacco

BOOKER'S
DISTILLER: Jim Beam

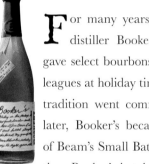

For many years, Jim Beam master distiller Booker Noe (1929–2004) gave select bourbons to friends and colleagues at holiday time, and in 1988 this tradition went commercial. Four years later, Booker's became the centerpiece of Beam's Small Batch Bourbon Collection. Booker's is taken from the "center cut" of warehouses, those locations in the middle of buildings that are less susceptible to heat and cold and can therefore provide a more consistent form of aging. In F. Paul Pacult's book *American Still Life*, Noe says, "I select from these central areas because I know from experience that the whiskeys in the seven-to-eight-year range will be oaky and vanilla-like, robust but smooth." The whiskey is bottled straight from the barrel, uncut and unfiltered. So the proof level of Booker's varies from one bottling to another, and the whiskey has all the nuance that nature gives it. For many who love full-flavored bourbon, Booker's boasts the same kind of vivid personality as Noe himself.

Age 6–8 years
Proof 121–127
Color deep amber
Aroma oak, vanilla, smoky charcoal
Flavor an intense combination of fruit, tannin, and tobacco

BULLEIT
DISTILLER: Four Roses

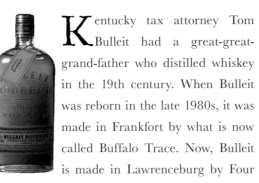

Kentucky tax attorney Tom Bulleit had a great-great-grand-father who distilled whiskey in the 19th century. When Bulleit was reborn in the late 1980s, it was made in Frankfort by what is now called Buffalo Trace. Now, Bulleit is made in Lawrenceburg by Four Roses, and the brand is owned by Diageo.

Age no age statement
Proof 90
Color russet
Aroma rich, oaky
Flavor hints of vanilla and honey

 CLASSIC CASK
DISTILLER: Not available

This bourbon is bottled by Even Kulsveen of Kentucky Bourbon Distillers for the brand's owner, Alan Shayne, who also operates the Scotch Malt Whisky Society of America. The whiskey was introduced in 2005.

Age 13 years
Proof 90.8
Color mahogany
Aroma vanilla, charred oak, toffee, honey
Flavor honey, maple, toffee, spice—dry

 CORNER CREEK
DISTILLER: Not available

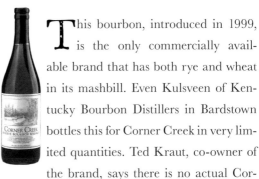

This bourbon, introduced in 1999, is the only commercially available brand that has both rye and wheat in its mashbill. Even Kulsveen of Kentucky Bourbon Distillers in Bardstown bottles this for Corner Creek in very limited quantities. Ted Kraut, co-owner of the brand, says there is no actual Corner Creek, although an illustration of a stream adorns the label. "Corner Creek is a figment of my imagination," he jokes. "We decided to make a sit-down, sipping whiskey. You can visualize yourself by a slow-running stream, fishing, and relaxing with our whiskey."

Age 8 years
Proof 88
Color amber
Aroma vanilla, brown sugar, oak, caramel, maple
Flavor caramel, brown sugar, vanilla, oak, leather

EAGLE RARE
DISTILLER: Buffalo Trace

This brand was first introduced by Seagram's in the 1970s.

Age 10 years
Proof 90
Color amber
Aroma oak, vanilla, brown sugar, caramel, hazelnut
Flavor oak, vanilla, brown sugar, caramel, hazelnut, soft mint

Age 10 years (single barrel)
Proof 90
Color amber
Aroma sweet caramel, vanilla
Flavor rich caramel, toast, marzipan, white pepper

Age 17 years
Proof 90
Color amber with gold streaks
Aroma vanilla, molasses, maple, spice
Flavor vanilla cream, maple syrup, molasses, candied fruit, leather, cinnamon, mint

ELIJAH CRAIG
DISTILLER: Heaven Hill

Elijah Craig (1743–1808) was a Baptist preacher who emigrated from Virginia to Kentucky and began distilling. Over the years many have claimed that Craig was the first to make bourbon, and many others have claimed that it was important for those fighting the temperance movement to argue that Kentucky's spirits flowed from a man of the cloth. There is no connection between the whiskey made by Craig and the whiskey now made in his name.

Age 12 years
Proof 94
Color deep copper
Aroma vanilla, sweet fruit, mint
Flavor spice, oak, char smoke, dry wood

Age 18 years (single barrel)

Proof 90

Color medium amber, burnt orange

Aroma crisp oak, nut—weighty

Flavor dry vanilla—complex, round, and toasty

ELMER T. LEE
DISTILLER: Buffalo Trace

Elmer T. Lee joined the George T. Stagg Distillery in the late 1940s as an engineer and worked his way through various jobs as the facility became the Albert B. Blanton Distillery in 1953, then the Ancient Age Distillery in 1962, and the Buffalo Trace Distillery in 2001. Lee created the first single-barrel product of modern times in 1984, and this bourbon was named after him in 1992, in honor of his "retirement" (he still comes to the distillery on a regular basis). Barrels that become Elmer T. Lee are generally about ten years old.

Age no age statement (single barrel)

Proof 90

Color amber

Aroma caramel, cereal, vanilla, candied fruit

Flavor cereal, caramel, vanilla, soot

EVAN WILLIAMS SINGLE-BARREL VINTAGES
DISTILLER: Heaven Hill

Another of the leading candidates for the first person to make bourbon, Evan Williams started distilling commercially in Louisville in 1783—although he seems to have done it without the necessary permit for at least five years. Williams showed another type of rugged individualism by bringing his whiskey to town meetings, where it was met with considerable criticism. By 1802, faced with complaints from neighbors, Williams's distillery went out of business. There is no relation between the whiskey once made by Williams and the whiskey now produced in his name. Heaven Hill began bottling whiskeys with specific vintages in 1994, with a bottling that had been aged for eight years. By 2005 the company had released seven more vintage whiskeys, with more to come. Here are two recent examples.

Age 11 years (1994 vintage)

Proof 86.6

Color bright amber-bronze

Aroma pepper, mint, dark fruit, oak, resin

Flavor spice, apple, mint, caramel, almonds—oily, smoky, and dry

Age 10 years (1995 vintage)

Proof 86.6

Color copper

Aroma cereal, toffee, vanilla, dried fruit, herbs, flowers

Flavor spice, cereal, grapefruit, black pepper, flowers

EXPERIMENTAL COLLECTION
DISTILLER: Buffalo Trace

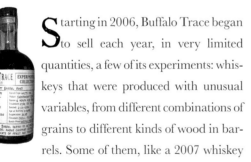

Starting in 2006, Buffalo Trace began to sell each year, in very limited quantities, a few of its experiments: whiskeys that were produced with unusual variables, from different combinations of grains to different kinds of wood in barrels. Some of them, like a 2007 whiskey that spend some time in wood that formerly housed chardonnay, was a bourbon, but not a straight bourbon, which can only be aged in wood that has never been used before. Here are notes for the Fire Pot Barrel, a 2006 straight bourbon that was aged in wood heated to 102 degrees for 23 minutes, more of a burn than is normally used for a bourbon barrel.

Age 10 years

Proof 90

Color amber chestnut

Aroma smoky

Flavor hints of fruit and tobacco

EZRA B.
DISTILLER: Not available

The name Ezra Brooks—and the cute nickname Ezra B.— was created by marketers to give an impression of the Old South. The bourbon is bottled in Kentucky for a Missouri company.

Age 12 years

Proof 99

Color amber

Aroma toasted nuts and wood

Flavor rich and full bodied, with a slightly fruity sweetness

FOUR ROSES SINGLE BARREL
DISTILLER: Four Roses

Coming out of Prohibition, Four Roses was the best-selling whiskey in America. It continued to be a dominant brand up to the Kennedy administration. In the early 1960s it was taken out of the

U.S. market and turned into an overseas brand. Huh? Well, the brand's disappearance was the result of shifting priorities. Four Roses was bought just after World War II by the Canadian booze company Seagram's, which took in enormous profits by selling blended whiskys. While the spirits made by Four Roses were useful for Seagram's blends, the company did not consider Four Roses' straight bourbon important. Only in 2003, under the ownership of the Kirin Brewery in Japan, did the brand start to be reintroduced, very slowly, into the U.S. market.

Age 7 years
Proof 100
Color amber
Aroma honey, fruit, maple, spice
Flavor fruity, floral, plus notes of honey and maple syrup and hints of cinnamon and nutmeg—mellow and smooth

 GEORGE T. STAGG
DISTILLER: Buffalo Trace

According to Sam K. Cecil in *The Evolution of the Bourbon Whiskey Industry in Kentucky*, George T. Stagg was "a not-too-trustworthy friend" to E. H. Taylor, who owned the distilling

operation that would eventually become Buffalo Trace. Stagg loaned money to Taylor in the mid-1880s and then foreclosed, taking over Taylor's company. Stagg did well but died less than ten years later. This whiskey is bottled at barrel proof, around 140, which makes it the strongest bourbon on the market.

Age 15 years (single barrel)
Proof 137.6
Color Deep copper
Aroma Butterscotch, toffee, cherry, vanilla, oak, marzipan
Flavor Butterscotch, sweet corn, toasted marshmallow, marzipan, oak, tobacco, leather, spice

 **HANCOCK'S PRESIDENT'S RESERVE**
DISTILLER: Buffalo Trace

The bourbon is named for Hancock Taylor, the great-uncle of President Zachary Taylor and one of the earliest surveyors of Kentucky, who was killed by Native Americans in 1774. His will, written just before he died from a gunshot wound, was one of the first legal documents executed in the territory. Barrels that become Hancock's are generally about ten years old.

Age no age statement (single barrel)
Proof 88.9
Color copper
Aroma honey, spice, tropical fruit
Flavor honey, cereal, orange zest, spice

 HENRY McKENNA
DISTILLER: *Heaven Hill*

 Irish immigrant Henry McKenna began distilling in Kentucky in 1855, and his whiskey was very popular in the late 19th century. McKenna died in 1893, and his distillery was shuttered by Prohibition. Although his descendants reopened the facility after Repeal, they sold the place to Seagram's in 1941, and the whiskey was discontinued. Heaven Hill later purchased the brand name but not the recipe.

Age 10 years (single barrel)
Proof 100
Color deep golden amber
Aroma charcoal, sweet citrus, sweet maple,

pepper
Flavor caramel, charcoal, mint, with a spicy, dry finish

 JEFFERSON'S
DISTILLER: *Not available*

 Introduced by McLain & Kyne in 2003

Age 8 years
Proof 88
Color amber
Aroma vanilla, caramel, fruit
Flavor vanilla, caramel, fruit

 JEFFERSON'S RESERVE
DISTILLER: *Not available*

 This was the first bourbon marketed by McLain & Kyne in 1998, and at that time it was a 15-year-old whiskey. Since then there have been different bottlings of this brand. The following information applies to the original bottling.

Age 15 years

Proof 90.2

Color deep amber

Aroma vanilla, raisin, caramel, butterscotch

Flavor vanilla, raisin, caramel, butterscotch

KENTUCKY VINTAGE

DISTILLER: Not available

This is one of the bourbons from Kentucky Bourbon Distillers, which has its own line of products and also creates whiskeys for a number of other companies.

Age 8 years

Proof 90

Color copper

Aroma deep vanilla, soft leather, flowers, butter

Flavor dark toffee, vanilla, butter, tobacco, soft leather, soot

KNOB CREEK

DISTILLER: Jim Beam

One of the three bourbons introduced in 1992, when Beam created the Small Batch Bourbon Collection, Knob Creek is named for one of Abraham Lincoln's boyhood homes, located

near Hodgenville, Kentucky. The president's father, Thomas, also allegedly worked at a distillery in the area.

Age 9 years

Proof 100

Color copper to medium amber

Aroma toasted nuts, grain, oak

Flavor sweet, woody, slightly fruity

 MAKER'S MARK

DISTILLER: Maker's Mark

This is the only "whisky" (they prefer the *e*-less spelling) made by this company, which took a major turn in 1954 by reformulating the bourbon they had been making for 20 years. Wheat is the secondary grain used in Maker's Mark.

Age no age statement

Proof 90

Color amber

Aroma honey, caramel, vanilla, dried fruit, light oak, black tea, plum, blackberry

Flavor honey, caramel, light oak, black tea, plum, dried fruit

COLLECTIBLES

The craze for bourbon decanters in the late 1970s produced a large—and somewhat strange—variety of bottles. A number of them commemorated individual states. Others saluted companies. A few honored fraternal organizations. One even marked the existence of King Kong.

Somehow, there wasn't one that recognized the importance of bottle collecting. "Jim Beam bottles were all the rage," says Terry Kovel, coauthor of the major guide to decanters *Kovels' Bottles Price List*. "The prices went crazy, and some of the bottles were going for thousands of dollars."

Then, almost inevitably, the mania for Beam bottles—and those issued by other distilleries, such as Wild Turkey, Old Fitzgerald, and Barton—went the way of Cabbage Patch Kids, Beanie Babies, and baseball cards.

In recent years decanters have made a slight comeback, says Kovel, who wrote the guide with her husband, Ralph. "The Jim Beam bottles that have something to do with golf have been gaining, but otherwise there's not much of a market for the ceramic decanters," she explains.

Far older collectibles can be pricey, too. The red amber bottle for United We Stand Old Bourbon Whiskey, produced between 1871 and 1883, has an estimated value of $3,100. In sharp contrast, a bottle of Old Bardstown Bourbon from 1978 that depicts the comedian Foster Brooks is worth only $20 to $28, while a Beam bottle celebrating the state of Arizona from 1968 usually goes for a mere $5.

The Kovels' guide gives prices for more than 12,000 bottles, with some pictured in black and white and a few in color. (A related Web site, www.kovels.com, lists prices for 500,000 more.) The book has a big bibliography, as well as a listing of collectible organizations, such as the Federation of Historical Bottle Collectors (www.fohbc.com).

Other whiskey-related memorabilia has collectible value, too—from promotional gewgaws such as tip trays used in bars to advertising of all sorts. "Anything that shows a flag, the Statue of Liberty, a naked woman, a car, or a plane," Kovel says, "has added value."

In whiskey advertising, it seems, some values never go out of style.

BEAM

No finer Whiskey in all this world!

❧ McAFEE'S ❧
BENCHMARK XO
DISTILLER: *Buffalo Trace*

This whiskey is named for the surveying company—which included surveyor Hancock Taylor (see "Hancock's President's Reserve")—that marked the land where Buffalo Trace's distillery now stands. Barrels that become McAfee's are about six to eight years old.

Age no age statement
Proof 94
Color medium amber
Aroma deep-roasted nut and caramel
Flavor full, balanced combination of nuts and caramel—creamy and stylish

❧ MICHTER'S ❧

DISTILLER: *Not available*

The name goes back to the last great distillery to make bourbon in Pennsylvania, but the whiskey in the bottle now hails from Kentucky. (See the entry on "A. H. Hirsch" for the whiskey made at Michter's but sold under a different name.)

Age 10 years
Proof 94.4
Color amber
Aroma caramel, vanilla, pear, cinnamon
Flavor caramel, vanilla, cinnamon, brown sugar, pear

❧ NOAH'S MILL ❧

DISTILLER: *Not available*

This bourbon has many siblings. The patriarch of this liquid family, Even Kulsveen, sells some of them, like this one, through his own Kentucky Bourbon Distillers in Bardstown. Other labels, including Corner Creek and Classic Cask, were created for other companies.

Age 15 years
Proof 114.3
Color deep copper
Aroma butterscotch, caramel, soft vanilla, cinnamon, cedar, pecan
Flavor butterscotch, vanilla, cinnamon, citrus, pecan, brown sugar, soot

OLD CHARTER

DISTILLER: Buffalo Trace

The brand, created in 1874, has had many owners; Sazerac, the parent company for Buffalo Trace, now controls it. The name refers to the Charter Oak, where the colonial charter for Connecticut was hidden from the British in 1687.

Age 8 years
Proof 80
Color light amber
Aroma caramel, vanilla
Flavor caramel, vanilla, spice

Age 10 years
Proof 86
Color amber
Aroma caramel, honey, vanilla, spice
Flavor caramel, honey, vanilla, spice, leather

Age 12 years (The Classic 90)
Proof 90
Color deep amber
Aroma caramel, honey, vanilla, spice
Flavor caramel, spice, honey, vanilla, lime

Age 13 years (Proprietor's Reserve)
Proof 90
Color amber
Aroma toffee, brown sugar, vanilla, hazelnut
Flavor toffee, brown sugar, vanilla, hazelnut

OLD EZRA
7-YEAR-OLD

DISTILLER: Not available

Like the other bourbon in this book sold by the David Sherman company—Ezra B.—this whiskey is named after a fictitious person invented for marketing purposes.

Age 7 years
Proof 101
Color amber
Aroma butterscotch, leather, and mint
Flavor vanilla, oak, and butterscotch; hint of mint

OLD FORESTER BIRTHDAY BOURBON

DISTILLER: Brown-Forman

To commemorate the birthday of the distillery's founder, George Garvin Brown, in 2002 Brown-Forman began to release special bourbons every September. In 2003 the company released two birthday bourbons. These are the bottlings introduced from 2002 to 2004.

Age 16 years (1989 vintage)
Proof 95
Color dark locust honey with an orange hue
Aroma dark chocolate, dried fruit, subtle vanilla, hints of pine and tobacco
Flavor soft oak, a subtle sweetness, nice fruit (apple) and spice character; hints of mint and chocolate

Age 15 years (spring 1990 vintage)
Proof 93
Color bright toffee with an orange glow
Aroma deep oak character; tobacco, spice, vanilla, and layers of dark fruit (raisins) mingle with dashes of black pepper
Flavor velvety notes of spice and intense

fruit are balanced with oak and sweet confectionary highlights

Age 15 years (fall 1990 vintage)
Proof 89
Color soft clover honey
Aroma softly sweet honeycomb notes mingle with subtle hints of orange, light vanilla, and faint traces of butterscotch and chocolate; a deep note of mint
Flavor subtle sweet notes of apple and citrus fade into a soft oak character; hints of dark fruit and aromatic spices

Age 10 years (1995 vintage)
Proof 94
Color chocolate-orange
Aroma oak, vanilla, black pepper, chocolate, maple, cinnamon
Flavor milk chocolate, nutmeg, mint, apple—sweet and intensely spicy

ᬳO L D R I Pᬳ
V A N W I N K L E
DISTILLER: Not available

Julian "Pappy" Van Winkle was a legendary master of bourbon, from his early days as a salesman at the Weller distillery around the turn of the 19th century up to his retirement in 1965 from running what had become the Stitzel-Weller distillery. When stockholders sold the place out from under his son, Julian Jr., in 1972, the family was left with this brand, which they revived with whiskeys that had been made at Stitzel-Weller. The company, now run by Julian III and his son Preston, offers a range of bourbons, all made with wheat. The Van Winkles established a joint venture in 2002 with Buffalo Trace. Because of the long time that bourbons spend in barrels, however, it will be several years before the Van Winkle line consists entirely of Buffalo Trace spirits.

Age 10 years

Proof 90

Color deep burnished copper

Aroma molasses, spice

Flavor sweet molasses, toffee, vanilla, brown spices, peppery rye, praline

Age 10 years

Proof 107

Color rich copper

Aroma spice, caramel, dried fruit, toasted nuts, honey

Flavor caramel-nut fudge, dried fruit, toasted nuts, peppery brown spices, floral honey

ᬳO L D W E L L E Rᬳ
A N T I Q U E
DISTILLER: Buffalo Trace

Made with wheat as a secondary grain, this is one of the brands formerly produced by the Stitzel-Weller distillery in Louisville.

Age 7 years

Proof 107

Color copper

Aroma deep toffee, caramel, vanilla, cherry, oak, yellow cake, butter brickle, marzipan

Flavor buckwheat honey, toffee, caramel, applesauce, vanilla, cherry, oak, butter, caramel corn

113

A Guide to the Bourbons

OLD WHISKEY RIVER

DISTILLER: *Heaven Hill*

Willie Nelson helped develop this bourbon, named after one of his songs, "Whiskey River," and formulated by Heaven Hill with his input. The brand, which helps raise money for charity, was created by a company called Alive Spirits. (It also worked on the Cabo Wabo tequila brand affiliated with rock singer Sammy Hagar.) Drinks Americas took over Old Whiskey River in 2002.

Age 6 years
Proof 86
Color light amber
Aroma vanilla, cereal, cherry, orange, pear, caramel, cinnamon
Flavor caramel, vanilla, cereal, orange, cherry, cinnamon

PAPPY VAN WINKLE'S FAMILY RESERVE

DISTILLER: *Not available*

This is part of the Van Winkle portfolio. (See "Old Rip Van Winkle.")

Age 15 years
Proof 107
Color hazy copper
Aroma caramel, toffee, brown spices, oak
Flavor intense caramel, toffee, and peppery brown spice; finishes with spice and wood notes

Age 20 years
Proof 90.4
Color deep amber, dark orange
Aroma leather, smoke, minerals, coffee, cigars
Flavor oiled leather, smoke, minerals, coffee, cigar box

PARKER'S HERITAGE

DISTILLER: Heaven Hill

This series of limited-edition bottlings, named for long-time master distiller Parker Beam—from a branch of the famous bourbon family that has made whiskey at Heaven Hill for going on seven generations—will release new spirits on an annual basis. The first in the series—a barrel-proof whiskey—is described here.

Age no age statement (but 12 years old)
Proof 122.6
Color deep copper
Aroma deep honey, butter brickle, cinnamon, vanilla, almond
Flavor vanilla, baked apple, cinnamon, cayenne pepper oak

POGUE MASTER'S SELECT

DISTILLER: Not available

The family behind this brand, the Pogues, have ancestors who distilled from the late

19th century. This whiskey, however, is produced by Even Kulsveen of Kentucky Bourbon Distillers in Bardstown, Kentucky.

Age 9 years
Proof 91
Color medium amber/pale bronze
Aroma maple, caramel, plum, confectioner's sugar
Flavor caramel, soft maple, buttered sweet corn

PURE KENTUCKY

DISTILLER: Not available

This is one of the bourbons produced and sold by Kentucky Bourbon Distillers, which is also a major bottler for other companies. (See "Pogue Master's Select," the previous listing.)

Age 10 years
Proof 107
Color amber
Aroma vanilla, leather, brown sugar, perfume
Flavor vanilla, soft leather, brown sugar, cereal

The brand takes its name from the Blanton family farm, which became the site of what is now the Buffalo Trace distillery. The Rock Hill Mansion, where the Blantons once lived, still remains on the Buffalo Trace property. This single-barrel brand was introduced in 1990.

Age no age statement

Proof 100

Color amber

Aroma caramel, vanilla, cinnamon, toasted almond

Flavor caramel, brown sugar, vanilla, cinnamon, corn syrup, toasted almond

Kentucky Bourbon Distillers sells this brand, as well as other bourbons, while also creating whiskeys that several other companies sell.

Age 12 years

Proof 100.1

Color deep amber

Aroma buckwheat honey, pear, vanilla, cinnamon

Flavor honey, vanilla, citrus (lemon, lime, bitter orange), caramel, cinnamon, molasses

SAM HOUSTON

DISTILLER: Not available

In 2003 this became the second whiskey to be sold by McLain & Kyne.

Age 10 years

Proof 90

Color deep amber

Aroma vanilla and caramel

Flavor vanilla and orange

1792 RIDGEMONT RESERVE

DISTILLER: Barton

When first introduced in 2004, this bourbon was called "Ridgewood Reserve." But after litigation between its maker, Barton, and Brown-Forman, the makers of Woodford Reserve, Barton was told to come up with a different brand name.

Age 8 years

Proof 93.7

Color deep copper with gold highlights

Aroma deep fruit notes (Granny Smith apples) rounded out by sweet vanilla

Flavor ripe fruit, oak, rich caramel—well rounded

VAN WINKLE SPECIAL RESERVE

DISTILLER: Not available

See entry for "Old Rip Van Winkle."

Age 12 years

Proof 90.4

Color brilliant amber-orange

Aroma toffee, caramel, nuts, brown spices

Flavor caramel, nuts, complex toffee, brown spices

VERY OLD JEFFERSON'S RESERVE

DISTILLER: Not available

Introduced by McLain & Kyne in 2003, this brand consists of very limited releases of longer-aged bourbons.

Age 17 to 25 years

Proof varies

Color varies

Aroma varies

Flavor varies

VERY SPECIAL OLD FITZGERALD

DISTILLER: Heaven Hill

Several owners—and more than 100 years—ago, Old Fitzgerald was presented as a whiskey for connoisseurs. Like its predecessors, this longer-aged version is made with wheat as the secondary grain.

Age 12 years

Proof 90

Color golden toffee

Aroma malt, leather, dry fruit

Flavor soft honey, vanilla, butterscotch—warm and balanced sweetness

VIRGINIA GENTLEMAN SMALL BATCH

DISTILLERS: Buffalo Trace and A. Smith Bowman

Introduced in the late 1990s, this bourbon is distilled once in Kentucky and then again in Virginia.

Age 6 years

Proof 90

Color deep amber

Aroma caramel, vanilla, a little oak

Flavor caramel, banana, nutmeg, and a lot of vanilla; leans to a sweetness

DISTILLER: Buffalo Trace

William LaRue Weller—depicted on the label of Old Weller—was the grandson of Daniel Weller, one of many pioneering distillers who ventured into Kentucky after the Whiskey Rebellion of 1794. W. L. Weller started his own whiskey-trading business after serving in the Mexican War. At the turn of the 19th century, Weller left his two sons in charge of the business, and shortly after that they began to work directly with the distilling Stitzel brothers, Frederick and A. Philip. By the end of Prohibition the two companies had merged as the Stitzel-Weller distillery. Julian "Pappy" Van Winkle (see "Old Rip Van Winkle"), who began selling for Weller in 1893, was the major force behind the company in the years following Repeal up until his retirement in 1965. The Weller brands—a range of bourbons made with wheat as the secondary grain—now belong to the Buffalo Trace portfolio.

Age 7 years (Special Reserve)
Proof 90
Color amber
Aroma honey, brown sugar, cherry, toffee, vanilla, leather
Flavor honey, brown sugar, toffee, leather, cherry, citrus, vanilla, chili pepper

Age 10 years (Centennial)
Proof 100
Color golden amber
Aroma toffee, caramel, brown sugar, plum, cherry oak, leather
Flavor toffee, caramel, brown sugar, cherry, leather, oak, citrus, spice, pipe tobacco

Age 12 years
Proof 90
Color amber
Aroma caramel, vanilla, cherry, honey
Flavor caramel, vanilla, cherry, black tea

W I L D   T U R K E Y

DISTILLER: Wild Turkey

Although the distillery has its roots with the Thomas B. Ripy family in the mid-19th century, the Wild Turkey brand was introduced as recently as the early 1940s by Thomas McCarthy, whose primary business, called Austin, Nichols, & Co. was food importing and distribution. Austin, Nichols, & Co. paid the Ripy operation to make the bourbon, and in 1970 it bought the distillery where Wild Turkey is still made.

Age 10 years (Russell's Reserve)
Proof 90
Color deep amber
Aroma oak and toffee
Flavor crisp, with sweet toffee and vanilla

Age no age statement (Rare Breed)
Proof 108.4
Color deep amber
Aroma spring flowers, black pepper, and almonds

Flavor assertive, with hints of orange, mint, and sweet tobacco; nutty, peppery, and toasty on the finish

Age no age statement (Kentucky Spirit)
Proof 101
Color deep amber
Aroma almonds, honey, tobacco
Flavor almonds, honey, blackberries, leather

Age 15 years (Tribute)
Proof 101
Color deep red amber
Aroma spice, nuts, vanilla, caramel
Flavor spice, nuts, vanilla, caramel

WOODFORD RESERVE

DISTILLER: Brown-Forman

Although the site of the Woodford Reserve Distillery has great historical importance—Dr. James Crow pioneered a more scientific method of distillation on these grounds—Brown-Forman began distillation here only in 1996. Then known as the Labrot & Graham Distillery, it became the first commercial distillery in decades to use pot stills. It was renamed the Woodford Reserve Distillery in 2004. This bourbon is a mixture of pot-still whiskeys made here and column-still whiskeys made at the company's plant in Louisville.

Age no age statement
Proof 90.4
Color bright, clear toffee
Aroma powerful vanilla overlays a fruit medley, sweet cocoa, and a dash of black-pepper spice
Flavor sweet crème brûlée and apricot tart

WOODFORD RESERVE DISTILLERY'S MASTER'S COLLECTION

DISTILLER: Brown-Forman

This series began in 2005 with the first whiskey made entirely in Woodford's pot stills. Four Grain bourbon (described below) was also notable for being the first bourbon in decades to be distilled from batches that included corn, barley, rye, and wheat. In 2007, the collection continued with a bourbon "finished" in chardonnay barrels.

Age no age statement (about 7 years)
Proof 94
Color medium honey
Aroma baking spices, sweet-tart fruit (apple, citrus), soft cocoa, vanilla, caramel, spearmint
Flavor soft vanilla, caramel, hints of spearmint, orange, pecans, delicate oak

BUFFALO TRACE
BUFFALO TRACE
BUFFALO TRACE
BUFFALO TRACE
BOURBON FLAVORED CARAMEL SAUCE
BUFFALO TRACE
BARBEQUE SAUCE

CHAPTER FIVE

THE TIES THAT BIND
Noses, Neats, and Mixology

Fine bourbon, like all works of art, is best appreciated on its own. Through the distiller's knowing craft and the barrel's unknowable impact, the collaboration of nature and nurture creates a wide range of flavors, aromas, and textures.

To best understand the personality of each whiskey, sample it straight, or judiciously apply an ice cube or a splash of water.

Sure, you could pour bourbon over a glass filled with ice, and you could add a healthy slug of water. But the prudent sampler will proceed with caution. Begin by pouring an ounce of the whiskey into a clear glass and holding it up to the light to catch the spirit's color. Brown and red and gold will each be present in different measures, with the hues varying from one bourbon to the next.

Your sense of smell is crucial to your sense of taste. Your nose, especially a few sensitive areas high in the nasal cavity, can sniff out thousands of aromas, while your tongue can distinguish only four tastes: sweet, sour, salty, and bitter. Don't hesitate to sniff and think, think and sniff, until you've determined what an aficionado would call the "nose" of the whiskey.

So poke your actual nose—meaning the thing on the front of your face—over the edge of the glass and take a sniff. Pause. Think about what you're detecting. Cereal? Maple? Smoke? Something else? Now stick your nose into the glass. Sniff again. Pause. Think some more. If you detected spice, try to figure out which one. Cinnamon? Nutmeg? Pepper? Now keep your mouth open and take a deeper breath. Pause. Think again. Try to figure out the subtle elements that make up the whole. What kind of fruit? Citrus? What kind of citrus? Orange?

By this time you should be more than ready to take a little sip. Do just that, swishing the liquid around in your mouth. Turn your mind over to the impressions being created. Is the bourbon fiery? Do you taste the sweetness of corn? Does the whiskey have a particular consistency? It may help to close your eyes. After you swallow, take a quick breath through your mouth so that the vapors reach back to those sensitive areas in your nasal cavity.

If the bourbon seems quite strong, and if the aromas and flavors seem to be in a tight cluster, try adding a splash of mineral water. This can help to "open up" the bourbon, so that the sensations are softer and more diffuse. Many distillers dilute their whiskeys by up to 50 percent—as much water as whiskey—when assessing their specific personalities.

But your goal, of course, is pleasure. Experiment with different amounts of water, and try adding an ice cube or two as an alternative. Find out what combination works best for you. You might end up drinking delicate spirits straight while pouring a healthy splash into those with robust character.

Mixers can enhance the flavors of bourbon, but they have the potential for masking some of them as well. With a less expensive whiskey, which may have less complexity, adding cola may not cost you much in the way of flavor. But if you've spent a considerable amount of money on something distinctive, adding a mixer could make it harder to appreciate the whiskey's particular charms.

Master distillers go to a lot of time and trouble to produce these treasures, and they are reluctant to advise consumers to use more than a little water or ice. But they understand that different people have different tastes. "If you want to add a little ginger ale to your bourbon," says Wild Turkey master distiller Jimmy Russell, "go ahead and add a little ginger ale."

Cocktails can be even trickier than mixers. Some would argue—and they have a very good point—that the richness and complexity of high-end whiskey can be overpowered by other ingredients in a mixed drink. Yet with the exploding popularity of the mixed drink, there are ways to enjoy finer bourbons in libations both old and new.

You should feel free to save the good stuff for straight sipping and use a less expensive bourbon for cocktails. The choice, of course, is yours. What follow are just a few of the many concoctions featuring our favorite spirit.

❧ MINT JULEP ❧

The julep is now associated almost entirely with bourbon, but this was not always so. The 1862 edition of *The Bar-Tender's Guide* by Jerry Thomas, the first significant compiler of cocktail recipes, lists five different kinds of julep, including the whiskey julep, and his mint-julep recipe calls for brandy.

The Thomas book frames a debate that continues to split mint-julep lovers: to crush or not to crush the mint. If you use the mint simply as a garnish, you allow the bourbon to shine. If you gently press on the mint, however, you produce a mintier drink, which some love and some hate. I prefer a pronounced mint flavor and aroma, which you will get with this recipe adapted from *The Savoy Cocktail Book*, published in 1930.

SOUTHERN MINT JULEP

7 sprigs mint
½ tablespoon powdered sugar
3 ounces bourbon

Place four sprigs of mint leaves and sugar in a long tumbler, and crush together. (Try not to tear the leaves.) Add bourbon, and fill glass with cracked ice. Stir gently until glass is frosty. Garnish top with three more sprigs of mint.

For another, less traditional approach, try this recipe from the Web site of Maker's Mark:

"Mix over low heat a solution of equal parts sugar and water. Let cool. Choose 20 or 30 small mint leaves, preferably no larger than a dime, and put them in a small bowl. Pour 4 or 5 ounces of bourbon over them so they are covered. Let soak 5 minutes. Gather the leaves in a bunch in clean white cloth and wring them out into the bourbon. Dip the bunch back in the bourbon and wring them out again. Repeat several times.

"Mix the sugar solution and a liter of Maker's Mark bourbon—seven parts bourbon to two parts sugar solution. Now add the mint-infused bourbon, a tablespoon or less at a time, to the bourbon-and-syrup solution. After each addition you may need to leave the room to clear your nose. You want to add just enough of the minted bourbon so that the mixture has the faint smell of mint and tastes right. Stir thoroughly; you'll know when you've got it right.

"Add to a cup of ice crushed fine as snow but dry; do not allow it to degenerate into slush. Garnish with mint. Thus harmoniously blended by the deft touches of a skilled hand, the beverage is eminently appropriate for honorable men and beautiful women."

OLD-FASHIONED

Another cocktail, another debate. This drink, credited to the Pendennis Club of Louisville, Kentucky, generally comes with fruit, which some people crush (or "muddle") and others don't. In his book *The Craft of the Cocktail*, Dale DeGroff argues for muddling, so that the drink will be more than just sweetened whiskey. This is his version:

OLD-FASHIONED

1 teaspoon sugar

2 dashes Angostura bitters

2 orange slices

2 maraschino cherries

Water or soda water

2 ounces bourbon

In the bottom of an old-fashioned glass, carefully muddle the sugar, bitters, one orange slice, one cherry, and a splash of water or soda water. Remove the orange rind, and add the bourbon, ice, and more water or soda water. Garnish with the remaining orange slice and cherry.

Jerri Banks, a beverage consultant based in New York City, has come up with a variation (see next page) on the Old-Fashioned that gets its name from the use of dried fruits available during the cold season. "I love whiskey," Banks says,

"but I know that many neophyte palates find it too strong. This combination of dried fruits softens that intensity by creating a bridge to the classic old-fashioned—with its cherry, bitters, and orange components—with dried fruits and ginger."

Winter-Fruit Smash

2 ounces Spiced Fruit Mixture (recipe below)

1½ ounces Maker's Mark bourbon

1 ounce lemon juice

Dash Angostura bitters

Orange twist

Muddle spiced fruits gently in mixing glass. Add whiskey, lemon juice, bitters, and ice. Shake well and pour entire mixture into an old-fashioned glass. Garnish with orange twist.

Spiced Fruit Mixture

2 cups simple syrup (equal parts hot water and sugar, stirred until dissolved)

1 cup candied ginger

1 cup dried sour cherries

1 cup dried apricots, quartered

1 cinnamon stick

3–4 star anise

Make simple syrup. Pour warm syrup over fruits and spices. Steep for a minimum of 24 hours before using.

This combination of dried fruits softens the Old-Fashioned's intensity by creating a bridge to the classic cocktail—with its cherry, bitters, and orange— with dried fruits and ginger.

The best story, whether true or not, is that Winston Churchill's mum, Jennie, threw a party for Samuel Tilden in 1874 when he was elected governor of New York. On this occasion, a bartender at the Manhattan Club created a cocktail that was made with rye whiskey, it seems. Nowadays the type of whiskey used varies from rye to Canadian to Kentucky's finest.

MANHATTAN

2 ounces bourbon

1 ounce sweet vermouth (the red stuff, a.k.a. Italian

vermouth)

2 dashes Angostura bitters

1 maraschino cherry

Combine first three ingredients in a mixing glass with ice, and stir until chilled. Strain into a cocktail glass and garnish with the cherry.

Here is a less sweet variation:

THE PERFECT MANHATTAN

2 ounces bourbon

½ ounce sweet vermouth

½ ounce dry vermouth (the off-white stuff,

a.k.a. French vermouth)

2 dashes Angostura bitters

Lemon twist

Combine first four ingredients in a mixing glass with ice, and stir until chilled. Strain into a cocktail glass and garnish with lemon twist.

CASSIS COCKTAIL

This drink, from the 1947 *Bartender's Guide* by "Trader Vic Bergeron" takes the Manhattan to a deeper, fruitier level.

2 ounces bourbon
1 ounce dry vermouth
2 teaspoons crème de cassis

Shake all ingredients over ice, and strain into a cocktail glass.

WILD TURKEY PRESBYTERIAN

The following recipe comes from the Wild Turkey Web site (www.wildturkeybourbon.com), but that doesn't mean that master distiller Jimmy Russell would endorse the use of his more expensive whiskey in it. In fact, this cocktail can be made with any denomination of bourbon. As for the reason why this particular combination was named after a church, well, the story has been lost, so God only knows.

1½ ounces Wild Turkey bourbon
1 ounce ginger ale
1 ounce club soda
Lemon twist

Pour Wild Turkey in a tall glass over ice. Add equal parts ginger ale and club soda. Stir gently. Garnish with lemon twist.

WARD EIGHT

Few cocktails have such a great back story as the Ward Eight. The name of this drink comes from a political district in Boston that Martin Lomasney ruled from the 1880s to the 1920s. Lomasney, who was given the nickname "The Mahatma" by a local paper, was so confidently in charge that in 1898 on the night *before* an election, he and his supporters had a victory party at a downtown restaurant, where the drink was born. Strangely enough, Lomasney was a teetotaler, so it's possible that he never enjoyed this cocktail himself. The original drink was made with rye whiskey, but this version substitutes Basil Hayden's, a bourbon with a high rye content.

2 ounces Basil Hayden's bourbon

¾ ounce lemon juice

¾ ounce orange juice

1 teaspoon grenadine

½ teaspoon simple syrup

Shake all ingredients over ice, and strain into a cocktail glass.

HORSE'S NECK

In his 1948 book, *The Fine Art of Mixing Drinks*, David Embury called this the "great what-is-it of the Highball tribe," referring to the cocktail's origins as a simple whiskey-and-mixer combo and its later incarnations as a nonalcoholic libation and as a gin drink. Because this is a book about bourbon, here the Horse's Neck features that spirit. The recipe requires a rather long piece of lemon peel, set as a spiral that circles inside a Collins glass with one end draping over the lip and resembling, in shape, the neck of a horse.

2–3 ounces bourbon

Lemon twist

Ginger ale

Pour bourbon into a Collins glass with three or four ice cubes and the artfully draped lemon twist. Fill with ginger ale.

COCKTAIL MAKING

For a more thorough appreciation of how to make cocktails, consult the books by Dale DeGroff, David Wondrich, Gary Regan, Mardee Haidin Regan, and Ted Haigh mentioned in the recipes. These people know their stuff, and they write with clarity and style. Learning from them is fun.

But here are a few basic guidelines to help you mix a delicious drink.

Use fresh juices. It's not that hard to squeeze a lemon, a lime, or an orange. A reamer is a handy tool, or you can try one of the many devices on the market for squeezing fresh juices. To make an orange (or lemon or lime) twist, use a paring knife to slice thin ovals about three-quarters of an inch by one and a half inches. Try not to get very much of the lighter-colored pith.

You'll get a colder cocktail, and one that's slightly less potent, if you break up the ice cubes before placing them in a shaker. Using a rolling pin or some other blunt instrument, whack the ice while it's in a canvas bag or still inside the plastic bag in which you bought it.

Measure, measure, measure. Professional bartenders who slop in ingredients willy-nilly often make awful cocktails. Some helpful equivalents: ¼ ounce equals 1 ½ teaspoons, ½ ounce equals 1 tablespoon, ¾ ounce equals 4 ½ teaspoons. A dash is about ten drops, or one good slug from a bottle with a plastic insert in the mouth that regulates pouring.

Chill the serving glass in the freezer before you start assembling ingredients, so that when you pour the drink it'll stay colder longer.

Simple syrup is, as the name suggests, easy to make. Place equal amounts of superfine sugar and water in a bottle, and shake. Come back in a little while and shake the mixture again. Keep doing this until all the sugar is dissolved. Refrigerate.

This contemporary creation by beverage consultant and *Esquire* magazine columnist David Wondrich, from his book *Killer Cocktails*, puts a delicately fruity spin on the lightness of Maker's Mark. (Other fine tipples with bourbon can be found in his book *Esquire Drinks*.)

2 ounces Maker's Mark bourbon
1 ounce Lillet White
1 teaspoon crème de cassis
2 dashes Peychaud's bitters
Lemon twist

Stir first four ingredients over ice in a mixing glass, and strain into a cocktail glass. Garnish with lemon twist.

137

Ted Haigh, who practices mixed-drink archaeology under the name of Dr. Cocktail, printed this recipe in his wondrous book *Vintage Spirits & Forgotten Cocktails.* He received word of the drink from Chuck Taggart, who runs a tasty Web site called The Gumbo Pages (www .gumbopages.com). Taggart learned of the recipe in an e-mail from a gentleman named Brooks Baldwin. "My grandmother, Mrs. Monte M. Lemann (born in New Orleans in 1895), inherited the recipe from her mother-in-law, Mrs. Lucien E. Lyons, shortly before the beginning of the First World War," Mr. Baldwin explained in the message. "As specified in the original recipe, my grandmother concocted this libation by the quart and stored it in an antique lead crystal decanter. Informed that science had linked lead crystal with lead poisoning, my grandmother said, 'It's a pretty bottle, so hush.'" Since this version of the recipe makes three drinks at a time, it could, appropriately, be shared by a married couple and a mother-in-law.

1 teaspoon Peychaud's bitters
1 teaspoon Angostura bitters
1 teaspoon Torani Amer liqueur
½ ounce curaçao
½ ounce simple syrup
½ ounce maraschino liqueur
3–4 dashes orange bitters
9 ounces bourbon

Shake all ingredients over ice, and strain into three cocktail glasses.

SEELBACH COCKTAIL

Gary Regan and Mardee Haidin Regan—stalwart chroniclers of the bourbon world in *The Book of Bourbon and Other Fine American Whiskeys* (1995) and *The Bourbon Companion* (1998), both sadly out of print—broke the code of silence over this wondrously spicy and fruity cocktail in their 1997 book, *New Classic Cocktails.* (The recipe is also available in Mardee Haidin Regan's 2003 book, *The Bartender's Best Friend.*) The world owes them a considerable debt of gratitude because you can now make this drink in the comfort of your own home, although sipping one at the Seelbach Hotel in Louisville, Kentucky, where the cocktail was born, is also a rare treat.

> *1 ounce bourbon*
> *½ ounce triple sec*
> *7 dashes Angostura bitters*
> *7 dashes Peychaud's bitters*
> *Chilled Champagne*
> *Orange twist*

Pour the bourbon, triple sec, and both bitters into a Champagne flute. Stir. Fill with Champagne and garnish with orange twist.

SOUTHERN CUCUMBER

This drink, from the Brazen Bean cocktail lounge in Portland, Oregon, is a more savory way to enjoy bourbon, and a wonderful change of pace from the common sweet-and-fruity approach.

½ cup seedless cucumber, diced into ½-inch pieces

½ ounce simple syrup

2 ounces bourbon

½ ounce lemon juice

½ ounce lime juice

2 ounces chilled ginger ale

Cucumber spear

Gently muddle the cucumber with the simple syrup in a mixing glass. Shake this over ice with the bourbon, lemon juice, and lime juice. Strain into a tall glass, top off with ginger ale, and garnish with a cucumber spear.

Many people, including lazy bartenders, use sour mix instead of fresh lemon juice.

❧ B O U R B O N   S O U R ☙

This simple classic doesn't get the respect it deserves, in part because so many people, including lazy bartenders, use sour mix instead of fresh lemon juice. And, I suspect, too many people go too sour, covering up the lovely sweetness of the whiskey.

2 ounces bourbon
½ ounce lemon juice
¼ ounce simple syrup

Shake all ingredients over ice, and strain into a cocktail glass.

❧ F R I S C O ☙

David Embury, an amateur chemist who became mixology's foremost lab technician, created a kind of periodic table of cocktails in *The Fine Art of Mixing Drinks* (1948). According to his taxonomy, the Frisco is a cocktail "based on the whiskey sour," meaning that it has the kind of relationship to the whiskey sour that neon does to helium—sort of. The addition of Bénédictine, a rather extravagant liqueur made by French monks, gives some vivid accents to the traditional bourbon sour. I have tweaked Embury's formula to highlight these accents.

1½ ounces bourbon
¾ ounce Bénédictine
¼ ounce lemon juice

Shake all ingredients over ice, and strain into a cocktail glass.

CHAPTER SIX

Touring the Bourbon Triangle

If you want to see how corn, rye, and barley get transformed into an amber elixir, there is just one place to go: Kentucky. It is the only place on Earth where grain goes in and straight bourbon comes out.

As a bonus, the state is flat-out beautiful, with its combination of that legendary bluegrass—thanks to the same limestone water that makes the whiskey so fine—and landscapes that move swiftly from rolling hills to steeper slopes.

At one time, distilleries could be found in many parts of the northern and western reaches of Kentucky, but now the number has dwindled to ten—operated by seven companies. Seven of these facilities offer tours—Barton plans to offer tours by 2009—and all of them are within easy driving distance of each other.

If you were to create a triangle with Louisville, Frankfort, and Bardstown as the three corners, it would—give or take a few miles—include all of these whiskey makers. (The only exception to this cluster is the A. Smith Bowman plant in Fredericksburg, Virginia, which does its own second distillation of spirits that have already been run through a still once in Frankfort.)

Touring the northeastern portion of this triangular area takes you through horse country, featuring exquisitely maintained farms outlined with white fences. To the south, a little past Bardstown, you encounter a distinctive kind of hill that's steep at the waist and round at the shoulders: the knob. One bourbon, Knob Creek, is named for the place where Abraham Lincoln lived as a boy before his family moved to Indiana and near where his father, Thomas, may have worked in a distillery.

Visiting one distillery does not mean that you have visited them all. Each place has its own character, from the look of the buildings to the way the whiskey is made. And the end of a tour almost always brings a reward, which could be a sample of bourbon, for those 21 or older, or a piece of candy flavored with the spirit. Most distilleries do not offer tours on major holidays. Call ahead to make sure you can be accommodated.

The Kentucky Department of Tourism provides good information about distilleries that are open to the public at its Web site (www.travel.ky.gov). And the Web site of the Kentucky Distillers' Association (www.kybourbon.com) has tourist information and a map that describes what it calls the Bourbon Trail. There is no fixed starting or finishing point—you can begin at any of seven distilleries and then mosey on down the road. It shouldn't take more than an hour or so at most to drive from one place to another.

The following route is only one of many that you could choose. It starts in the state's capital, Frankfort, which is about 50 miles east of Louisville and about 25 miles west of Lexington.

If you were to create a triangle with Louisville, Frankfort, and Bardstown as the three corners, it would— give or take a few miles— include all of these whiskey makers.

If you visit the distilleries located in Versailles and Frankfort, you go through Thoroughbred-horse country, where most of the prominent racing stock in the United States is bred and sold.

❧ BUFFALO TRACE ☙

1001 Wilkinson Boulevard

Frankfort, Kentucky 40601

(502) 696-5926

(800) 654-8471

www.buffalotrace.com

Tours conducted year round

The first modern distillery on this 110-acre site in the city of Frankfort was built in 1857, and among the innovations back then was the use of steam heat to cook the grains, distill the spirits, and warm the warehouses where whiskey was being aged. More than 100 buildings now grace the neatly trimmed grounds, with a water tower that rises to 170 feet and displays an image of the distillery's trademark buffalo. The four-story still house contains three operating stills and 12 fermentation tanks, and the warehouses are formed by massive wood beams and clad by red brick. The two-story clubhouse, made of 200-year-old logs from old Kentucky cabins, is available for special groups, and all visitors end their tours of the facilities at the reception area and gift shop.

The distillery is named for the buffalo tracks along a nearby river that became pathways for human settlers, so the company honored this heritage by putting the creature on its water tower, where it looms over the facility and its grounds.

KENTUCKY
BOURBON FESTIVAL

Bardstown, Kentucky, calls itself the Bourbon Capital of the World, and the town takes this slogan so seriously that it registered it as a trademark. Each year, during the third week of September, Bardstown celebrates the whiskey with the Kentucky Bourbon Festival.

The event, which began in 1992 and now spans five days, draws more than 40,000 people each year. In addition to tastings of bourbon, recent fests have included free concerts, a whiskey seminar, barrel relay races, dances, walking tours of the city, a chili cook-off, a golf tournament, and a gala party. Find information about the festival at www.kybourbonfestival.com.

⊱ WOODFORD ⊰ RESERVE

7855 McCracken Pike
Versailles, Kentucky 40383
(859) 879-1812
www.woodfordreserve.com

The path to the Woodford Reserve distillery winds around horse farms near the town of Versailles (pronounced ver-SALES) and ends up alongside Glenn's Creek. The buildings on this 72-acre site, designated a National Historic Landmark in 2000, have been restored recently and complemented by new structures and equipment. Here, when the operation was known as the Oscar Pepper Distillery, Dr. James Crow introduced and perfected some of the techniques, such as the sour-mash process, that would become universal in the bourbon industry. It is the only whiskey distillery in the United States that uses copper pot stills. You may choose from three separate tours that emphasize different aspects of the distillery, such as the whiskey-making process or the architectural and cultural history of the site. Lunch is available from April to October, and a large gift shop has general merchandise as well as items with the Woodford Reserve logo.

A former distillery on the site of Woodford Reserve was the place where Dr. James Crow worked hard to develop many of the practices that are now common, and now the property has been renovated and updated for use today.

AMERICAN
WHISKEY TRAIL

Bourbon dominates the American Whiskey Trail, a set of travel destinations that show the distilling heritage of the United States. First and foremost is the George Washington distillery, a reconstruction project at our first president's Mount Vernon home and farm. Washington was one of the biggest distillers—mostly making rye whiskey—in the new United States. The trail also leads to bourbon distilleries in Kentucky; whiskey operations in Tennessee; and other historic locations, such as Woodville Plantation in Bridgeville, Pennsylvania, a significant site related to the Whiskey Rebellion of 1794. The American Whiskey Trail was created by the Distilled Spirits Council, a trade organization that has been a source of funds for the Mount Vernon reconstruction. For more information, go to www.americanwhiskeytrail.com.

Take a look around the Wild Turkey distillery, and you'll know that you're in farming country—the buildings on the grounds here have not been gussied up, reflecting the no-nonsense approach to whiskey that is honored here.

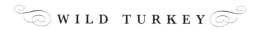
You can truly understand the agrarian roots of the whiskey business at this facility along the Kentucky River, which bears a distinct resemblance to the farms and silos found in many small towns in America's heartland. (Of course, this *is* a place that processes corn, rye, and barley.) The stillhouse could be mistaken for a grain elevator, and the many warehouses for buildings that house crops rather than bourbon in the making. Visitors can see the 40-foot-tall column turning distiller's beer into clear spirit, observe the pouring of this "white dog" into new barrels, peek into warehouses with thousands of barrels, and watch as the finished bourbon is put into bottles. The modest-sized gift shop is yet another indication that the distillation of spirits is the primary goal here. The distillery is closed the first full week of January and the last two full weeks of July; at other times of the year, you should call ahead to make sure the plant will be in full swing when you visit. Tours generally begin at 9:30 and 10:30 a.m. and at 12:30 and 2:30 p.m.

FOUR ROSES

1224 Bonds Mill Road

Lawrenceburg, Kentucky 40342

(502) 839-3436

www.fourroses.us

The Four Roses distillery may be located just a few minutes from Wild Turkey, but the style of the facility is half a continent away. The main buildings, completed in 1911, were designed by a Louisville architect in the Spanish Mission style found in the western United States. Tours start in the visitor center and gift shop, which opened in 2004. After checking out interactive exhibits on bourbon and viewing a 15-minute film on the history of Four Roses and whiskey production, visitors begin at the towering grain silo and follow the process all the way to the final stage of bottling. Along the tour, they get to see one of the distinctive parts of the Four Roses operation: the single-story warehouses used to bring its products to maturity. Tours, which last about 45 minutes, are given Monday through Saturday from 9 a.m. to 4 p.m.

There is an exotic feel to the Four Roses buildings, unlike any other facility devoted to bourbon, thanks to the architect who in the early 20th century thought this rural-area Kentucky operation needed a touch of Spanish Mission style.

You can learn about the aging and bottling of bourbon at Heaven Hill's visitor center in Bardstown, but the company actually produces its new spirit in Louisville (lower left), because a fire wiped out the stillhouse in Bardstown back in 1996.

HEAVEN HILL

1311 Gilkey Run Road
Bardstown, Kentucky 40004
(502) 337-1000
www.bourbonheritagecenter.com

There are no distillery tours at the Heaven Hill facility, for the simple reason that there is no Heaven Hill distillery in town. In 1996 a massive fire wiped out the distilling operation and several nearby warehouses. While many warehouses survived the disaster, Heaven Hill had to make other arrangements for spirit production, so in 2000 the company bought the Bernheim Distillery in Louisville. But Heaven Hill continues to fill barrels, age barrels, and bottle whiskey in Bardstown, where the company's Bourbon Heritage Center opened in 2004. This building is constructed of materials that are important in whiskey making: copper (used to make equipment), limestone (the natural filter for water), and white oak (the required wood for barrels). And the shape of the center resembles that of warehouses. Inside the building, interactive exhibits and a short film explain how bourbon is made, and there are displays of old ads and photographs. In the Taste of Heaven room—shaped like a barrel—visitors of legal drinking age can sample the company's products. The gift shop has crafts and merchandise bearing the Heaven Hill logo.

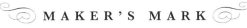

MAKER'S MARK

3350 Burks Spring Road

Loretto, Kentucky 40037

(270) 865-2099

www.makersmark.com

Visit Maker's Mark and you'll get the feeling of traveling back in time. All of the buildings, from the stillhouse to the tollhouse, have been beautifully restored to a Victorian splendor. The oldest distillery in the United States to have continuously made whiskey on its original site, this property was designated a National Historic Landmark in 1980. The grounds, with about 300 different types of plants, function as an arboretum as well as a whiskey-making facility. Visitors walk through the working distillery and view each part that helps convert grain into bourbon, from the copper mash kettles to the cypress fermentation vats to the wood-covered warehouses to the bottling lines, where women dip the necks of the bottles into red wax at a rapid clip. The gift shop has a wide variety of merchandise that reflects the red-topped Maker's Mark bottle, and people 21 and over can actually hand-dip their own souvenir bottles. Tours start every hour on the half hour from 10:30 a.m. to 3:30 p.m., Monday through Saturday. On Sundays, except for January and February, tours start at 1:30, 2:30, and 3:30 p.m.

Maker's Mark's grounds are impeccably maintained, from the Victorian-style buildings to the ever-upgraded arboretum, and visitors over the age of 21 can duplicate the distillery's trademark red-topped bottles by personally hand-dipping their own.

GETZ MUSEUM

Oscar Getz had a passion for whiskey—and just about anything connected to it. As the owner and operator of the Barton distillery from the 1940s until the 1980s, he collected hundreds of whiskey bottles, novelty decanters, old moonshine stills, advertising art, and much, much more. After Getz died in the early 1980s, his treasures were donated to the city of Bardstown, where they now reside in a 19th-century building that has been, at various times, a college seminary and a hospital used by both the Union and the Confederacy. The Oscar Getz Museum of Whiskey History has artifacts that span from the pre-Colonial era up to modern times. One room re-creates an old-time liquor store, with a wide range of rare whiskey bottles. (114 North Fifth Street, Bardstown, Kentucky 40004; (502) 348-2999)

JIM BEAM

149 Happy Hollow Road

Clermont, Kentucky 40110

(502) 543-9877

www.jimbeam.com

You can't actually see bourbon in the making at this Beam property, called the American Outpost, but a mini-museum describes the art of distillation and charts the seven generations of the Beam clan who have produced the best-selling bourbon in the world. (There's a short film that provides a lot of colorful detail as well.) Visitors can take a self-guided tour of the grounds to see a warehouse and a re-creation of a 19th-century barrel-making operation. More family memorabilia can be seen at the nearby T. Jeremiah Beam home, where samples of the company's Small Batch Bourbons are poured for those 21 and over (except on Sundays and election days). Beam merchandise is available in a small gift shop.

A small museum awaits near Clermont, which substitutes for an actual distillery tour, with a movie, historical exhibits, a facsimile of a cooperage, and a house next door that shows how the Beams lived and offers a nip to visiting adults.

THOROUGHBREDS AND REDHEADS WEEKEND

Two of Kentucky's best-known exports—bourbon and racehorses—come together each spring in a two-day event held by Maker's Mark in the city of Lexington and at the company's distillery outside the town of Loretto. In acknowledgment of the bourbon's distinctive look—the top of each bottle is dipped in bright red wax—this get-together is called Thoroughbreds and Redheads. Open to those who join the brand's Ambassador program—free to anyone 21 or older—the fun begins with the running of the Maker's Mark Mile on Friday at the Keeneland track in Lexington. That evening, Ambassadors attend a free party with music, a buffet, and giveaways (there is a nominal charge for alcoholic beverages). On Saturday the action shifts to the distillery, where there is an open house with tours of the facility and more free food. Ambassadors can purchase collectible bottles and go on the distillery's actual bottling line to dip them personally. And there is a rare opportunity to sample Maker's Mark in the making—whiskey straight from barrels that have not yet finished maturing.

INDEX

BIBLIOGRAPHY

Since this is a casual guide to bourbon, I haven't used footnotes, although throughout the book I have identified the sources of quoted material that doesn't come from my own interviews. The following books have been particularly useful. Some of them are out of print but can be found through used bookstores and Internet booksellers. All are essential reading for students of bourbon.

Carson, Gerald. *The Social History of Bourbon: An Unhurried Account of Our Star Spangled American Drink*. Dodd, Mead and Company, 1963.

Cecil, Sam K. *The Evolution of the Bourbon Whiskey Industry in Kentucky*. Turner Publishing, 1999.

Cowdery, Charles K. *Bourbon, Straight: The Uncut and Unfiltered Story of American Whiskey*. Made and Bottled in Kentucky, 2004.

Crowgey, Henry G. *Kentucky Bourbon: The Early Years of Whiskeymaking*. The University Press of Kentucky, 1971.

Gabányi, Stefan. *Whisk(e)y*. Abbeville Press, 1997.

Kellner, Esther. *Moonshine: Its History and Folklore*. The Bobbs-Merrill Company, 1971.

Kroll, Harry Harrison. *Bluegrass, Belles, and Bourbon: A Pictorial History of Whisky in Kentucky*. A. S. Barnes and Company, 1967.

Murray, Jim. *Classic Bourbon, Tennessee and Rye Whiskey*. Prion Books, 1998.

Pacult, F. Paul. *American Still Life: The Jim Beam Story and the Making of the World's #1 Bourbon*. Wiley, 2003.

Regan, Gary and Mardee Haidin Regan. *The Book of Bourbon and Other Fine American Whiskeys*. Chapters Publishing, 1995.

Regan, Gary and Mardee Haidin Regan. *The Bourbon Companion: A Connoisseur's Guide*. Running Press, 1998.

Samuels, Bill, Jr. *Maker's Mark: My Autobiography*. Saber Publishing, 2000.

The foremost American magazine on bourbon (and whiskey and beer) is *Malt Advocate* (www .maltadvocate.com), which is published in Emmaus, Pennsylvania. My description of barrel making was informed by a story from the January 2004 issue written by Lew Bryson called "How Wood You Like Your Bourbon?"

Another great source of information on bourbon (and other American whiskeys) is a newsletter out of Chicago called *The Bourbon Country Reader* (http://cowdery.home.netcom.com/page2.html).

Just as the interest in cocktails has shot way up, the number of informative and entertaining guides has increased dramatically. Here are some great books of recent vintage, as well as some old-timers worth seeking out.

Bergeron, "Trader Vic." *Bartender's Guide*. Doubleday and Company, 1947.

Craddock, Harry. *The Savoy Cocktail Book*. Simon and Schuster, 1930.

Crockett, Albert Stevens. *The Old Waldorf-Astoria Bar Book*. A. S. Crockett, 1935 (reprinted by the J. Peterman Company, 1998).

DeGroff, Dale. *The Craft of the Cocktail: Everything You Need to Know to Be a Master Bartender, with 500 Recipes*. Clarkson Potter, 2002.

Embury, David A. *The Fine Art of Mixing Drinks*. Doubleday and Company, 1958 (revised edition).

Haigh, Ted (aka "Dr. Cocktail"). *Vintage Spirits and Forgotten Cocktails*. Quarry Books, 2004.

Regan, Gary. *The Joy of Mixology*. Clarkson Potter, 2003.

Wondrich, David. *Esquire Drinks: An Opinionated and Irreverent Guide to Drinking*. Hearst Books, 2002.

Wondrich, David. *Killer Cocktails: An Intoxicating Guide to Sophisticated Drinking*. Harper Collins, 2005.